Centre for Learning Excellence

# Leading and Developing High Performance

by Dr Derek S Biddle

Bentley Jennison Publishing

**Leading and Developing High Performance**

**A Bentley Jennison Book**
Published by Bentley Jennison Publishing
1 Hollinswood Court, Stafford Park 1
Telford, Shropshire TF3 3DE
www.bentley-jennison.co.uk



ISBN 0-9554612-0-0
10 9 8 7 6 5 4 3 2 1

# foreword

By Ali Stewart, Bentley Jennison

"The purpose of Leading & Developing High Performance is not to promote the latest 'theory', nor is it a prescription for a universal panacea. Rather it shares successful methods of enabling people to meet the needs of the times."

Derek Biddle, PhD, MSc, CPsychol, AFBPsS, FIPB

High performance is 'caused to happen' by a leader rather than a mere manager.

**How are your leadership skills?**

*Leading & Developing High Performance* will help leaders to lead with strength and dignity, passion and compassion. It gives leaders a track to run on, taking them on a path from transactional to transformational leadership.

Becoming a high performing leader means new skills and behaviours have to be accepted, developed and mastered, it is a continuous learning process and we hope this book will set you on the right road ... enjoy the journey.

This book is supported by a full training programme and set of developmental diagnostic tools to help strengthen leadership capability. Research for the book has covered a diverse range of industries and market sectors, from central government to the largest commercial organisations, from small boat building companies and national timber suppliers to global chromium manufacturers, from the insurance industry to national utilities. The research has captured the essence of what the highest performing leaders across all these industries actually do on a day by day, week by week basis.

If you would like to know more please contact Bentley Jennison on **0845 675 0605** or e-mail **consulting@bentley-jennison.co.uk**

First published in 2006

# acknowledgments

I would like to acknowledge the help and support received from colleagues, particularly Dr Mike Carter, Joe Wainwright and Deepak Rughani, and also business friends whose enthusiasm sustained my own. There were many, but Richard Batley, Elaine Kennedy, Patrik von Sydow, Paul Walkinshaw and Dr Liz White deserve special mention.

In particular I would like to thank Ali Stewart whose unflagging support, determination and sheer hard work was the constant thread throughout.

Dr Derek S Biddle

# contents


| | | |
|---|---|---|
| chapter 1 | Background to the *Leading and Developing High Performance* Approach | 3 |
| chapter 2 | Underlying Attitudes and Beliefs for Success | 13 |
| chapter 3 | What High Performance Leader/Developers Actually Do | 41 |
| chapter 4 | Explicitness: The Under-Emphasised Skill | 73 |
| chapter 5 | Diagnosing Performance Issues<br>Why People Behave As They Do | 83 |
| chapter 6 | Rewards and Penalties | 109 |
| chapter 7 | Maximising People's Potential Through Feedback<br>Catch them doing it right | 125 |
| chapter 8 | Motivation<br>Different Strokes for Different Folks | 149 |
| chapter 9 | Situational Leadership and Consistency<br>Adapting Your Leadership Style Appropriately | 173 |
| chapter 10 | Leading Change & Transition | 195 |
| postscript | Putting It All Together | 209 |
| bibliography | | 213 |
| theories explained | | 215 |

**Leading and Developing High Performance**

# chapter 1

# Background to the *Leading and Developing High Performance* Approach



## Chapter Contents


- *Background to the Leading & Developing High Performance Approach*
- *Beyond Mere Management – The Results of High Performance Leadership*
- *The Leader/Developer Approach*
  - *Underlying Attitudes & Beliefs, Process, Skills and Change*
- *The New Competencies for Success*
- *Implications for the Leader/Developer*
- *Chapter Summary*

## Background to the *Leading & Developing High Performance* Approach

The genesis for this book came about through researching what effective managers, across a variety of industries, actually did when creating High Performance. 'Creating' is not too strong a term here because, in the same set of circumstances, some managers were highly effective, while many of their counterparts were much less so. It was as though some people had, in various ways, found an approach which really worked for them – and that approach was remarkably consistent across all the effective managers and range of industries – while the less successful managers operated to a much less cohesive or consistent approach.

What was sharply visible, too, was that the more effective managers were much more competent and comfortable in responding to the demands of today's organisational context, while the less effective ones, although perhaps having been successful in the past, were still struggling to come to grips with new ways of working.



We were encouraged, in the words of one of the people we worked with, to 'bottle' the best practice we found and thus make it available to others. Our experience since with thousands of managers is that they strongly identify with the approach, and find the techniques and practices meaningful, practical and readily applicable.

Whether your need is to fine tune your skills or cope well with a new set of circumstances, or whether you are becoming responsible for the performance of others for the first time, we hope, and sincerely believe, that sharing our approach with you will help.

# Beyond Mere Management – The Results of High Performance Leadership

The word 'management' is a very overused one. It is the term most often used to describe those people responsible for the work and performance of others. Management literature is full of definitions of the term, typical among which is 'The process of planning, organising, directing and controlling the work of organisation members and of using all available organisational resources to reach stated organisational goals'.

Such descriptions do not come anywhere near to describing what those people responsible for the work and performance of others *actually do when they are highly effective*. Moreover, much of the conventional theory and practices describe organisational life as it was, not as it is and will increasingly become. The times are not only "a changing", to quote the song, they have changed and will continue to do so. In other words, the context of so called management is radically different to what it was.



There is likely to be little argument that one of the imperatives in the millennium age is for High Performance; organisations, and the individuals within them, are unlikely to survive the fierce competitive climate otherwise. High Performance can be described in many ways, and certainly it is not just the effectiveness of doing the right things. This latter requires people at all levels to engage their judgement and use initiative responsibly.

One way of describing High Performance in a team setting is the following, which characterised all the High Performing Teams we studied. The first point to make was that ...

> ***...such results rarely happened by themselves, they were created; caused to happen by a Leader who was not a mere manager.***

As we will see, there was nothing magical about what such Leaders did, and often what they did was largely intuitive or carried out at an 'unconscious competence' level. Their approach and the skills required are readily shared and trainable, which is what this book is about.

## Results of High Performance Leadership

- ***Team all going in same Direction***

  *Have clear sense of purpose, can describe same vision but in their own words*
- ***High Morale and Involvement***

  *Feel positive about themselves, have Positive Regard for each other and Team Leader, strong sense of involvement and commitment to their work*
- ***High Achievement***

  *Purposeful, achieve highly above average standards of performance in quality and quantity*
- ***Meet Special Demands***

  *Deal with crises with vigour and resolution – see challenge, manage stress with fun and celebration*
- ***High Reputation***

  *Well known for service they provide and quality of their people, members tend to be promoted more and replacements keen to join*
- ***Manage Change***

  *Embrace change; take change in their stride and cope effectively with new situations*



Clearly this is not a sweat-shop situation, driven and compliant, but one with a momentum and impetus of its own. There is certainly high achievement, with very good output, attained through the purposeful use of energy, where there is meaning to what is to be achieved through an owned sense of purpose. There is some fun, 'snap, crackle and pop' about it, so that special demands are met, not with weariness and moaning, but with zest, vigour and challenge. Members feel confident about themselves and their contribution (even in lower level jobs), with high self-esteem, and also feel positive about other team members, including the Team Leader, where there is mutual respect and understanding.

Such teams gain a reputation for themselves, and individuals become successful within them and, sometimes, move on to better jobs, with the Leader being generous enough to welcome and encourage this, knowing that s/he can grow replacements. Such teams, too, cope well with change for they have formed the habit of learning and of continuous improvement. Above all, such a way of working is a more natural, fulfiling and psychologically healthy place to be than is commonly the case in many work situations.

The frameworks that follow stem from research and observation of what effective Leaders, across a variety of organisations and industries, actually do. As has been stressed, there was a remarkable consistency in what such people believe, carry out and carry through. Because many of these highly effective people were working at the 'unconscious competence' level, it was only by observing how they went about the job that it was possible to see what differentiated them from less effective performers. It was then possible to set this in a framework of solid, underpinning theory and practice, so that the whole approach could be made congruent and readily accessible to others.

It was evident that some people had found the approach and skills almost randomly, while others, perhaps equally well intentioned, hadn't – and they were much less effective as a result. Yet the approach and skills required are available to, and acquirable by, the vast majority of people who are responsible for the work of others, and this is our mission here.

# The Leader/Developer Approach

These highly effective people were *Leader/Developers*, which is the term we will use to describe them from now on. 'Leaders' in the sense that they did not just react to situations - they created the situation through their personal vision, energy and transformational skills. They made a difference, not just being content to maintain smoothly the status quo. 'Developers' in the sense that part of their vision was to see their people performing at their very best, enabling and stimulating them to become the best they could be, and doing whatever was necessary to bring this about.

All this may sound very charismatic and glamourous, requiring exceptional characteristics and skills. It isn't and it doesn't! What it does require, however, is committing to an approach as a way of life, working to a themed process consistently and systematically, and developing a set of skills which can be readily learned.



## Underlying Attitudes & Beliefs, Process, Skills and Change

- ***Underlying Attitudes & Beliefs***

  *These Leader/Developers have a key set of Underlying Attitudes & Beliefs, which they translate into practice through a Process and an associated set of Skills. More than anything else, the Underlying Attitudes & Beliefs matter; they provide the context, the rationale, the driving force for the whole. So important are these Underlying Attitudes & Beliefs, that they will be explored in detail in Chapter 2. They are based not on the* ***either/or principle****, but on the* ***both/and*** *one of High Challenge* ***and*** *High Support, where both apply in powerful and equal combination.*

- ***Process***

  *The Process gives a pathway, a systematic approach, a track to run on. This is particularly useful and important for those new, or relatively new, to the task of Leading and Developing High Performance. It provides a map or wiring diagram, as it were, where before there might only exist uncertainty or confusion.*

- ***Skills***

  *Many of the Skills which these highly effective Leader/Developers used are not generally given much emphasis in most management texts and training programmes. For example, Explicitness, Diagnosing Performance Issues, the subtle use of Rewards and Consequences, Visioning, etc, are rarely taught. Some of the skills required are more commonly dealt with – but are seldom taught as part of a total approach – and these we will spend less time on in order to concentrate on the crucial but less widely available ones. This will also allow more experienced managers to work from the base of what they already know.*

- ***Change***

  *Most importantly of all, these highly effective Leader/Developers we identified, were much better equipped to deal with a changing environment and in enabling their people to respond well to it. For the changing environment required not only working harder, but working differently in a way that such effective Leader/Developers were already carrying out very successfully. The mindset required, and the necessary Process and Skills to apply it is of crucial importance in responding to the vastly different environment of today, instead of the yesteryear for which the majority of managers were trained, and on which much management training is still focused. So, if competitive advantage is to come about through people, the way that competitive advantage is brought forth and used matters greatly. The Leader/Developers we describe, and their way of working, provide the key to this.*

# The New Competencies for Success

In the organisation context just described, there are a number of paradoxes. While operating this way is arguably a more natural psychologically healthy way of working and being, as well as a more productive one, many such changes have not fulfiled what was expected of them, or have proved difficult to implement. One reason for this is because many managers felt or feel threatened by this way of working – what is their job and what skills do they have in all this? It requires a different set of competencies to those which they have perhaps become used to. The requirement, simply stated, is to become a Leader/Developer.

For some employees, too, the new context was and is experienced as more work, more hassle, more stress, with greater fulfilment and reward. To understand why, for the moment, let us use an analogy....



> *Many people have experienced the new requirements, often suddenly placed upon them, as similar to being placed on top of a skyscraper without a parapet or railings, in the dark, and being asked to roller skate to intricate patterns. The response would be to huddle in the safe territory of the middle of the roof – the risks being too great otherwise. If, on the other hand, boundaries are defined, everything is well lit and skills are honed, then it is another matter indeed – the adventurous resourcefulness and skills displayed can be awesome.*

While some have responded very positively to the new opportunities, others have perhaps used their newly released initiative irresponsibly; the Team Leader is left with a confusingly wide range of responses to deal with, whereas before there was more comfortable and controllable uniformity.

The point is, that to create a High Performing Team in this new situation, requires a different or additional set of competencies, founded on a particular mindset or paradigm. It is this which the highly effective Leader/Developers we worked with were operating to so successfully, and in a way which was significantly different from the average, or marginally performing, managers. Moreover, our findings have been replicated by many other studies across all types of organisations – manufacturing, sales, retailing, financial services, governmental, etc. What we have sought to do is to operationalise them and make them accessible. For they are readily learned, and will benefit anyone responsible for leading others to improve their own performance.

# Implications for the Leader/Developer

Much of what we have to say can be seen as common sense, hopefully in a way whereby much of the fog which confuses the issues of Leading & Developing High Performance can be dispersed. We take the view that if common sense approaches to the ways in which people can better meet challenges – be successful and thrive, become '*the best they can be*', be more fulfiled and work better together – can be learned and applied, then this should be a cause for celebration not scepticism.

The oddity for us is that the essentially authentic and common sense approach that such effective Leader/Developers take, should be so **unusual**. There is no magic in their success and the people involved are a not a newly discovered breed of super heroes. They are down to earth people who have **learned** the most effective ways of dealing with organisational issues and have created their own, and enabled their people's, success.



The approach we have taken is to make accessible what such people actually do by linking together behavioural models, which reflect best practice, into an overall process. Our intent has been to do this in a way in which they can be both understood and applied, and which creates connections with people's own practical experience.

The purpose of *Leading & Developing High Performance* is not to promote the latest 'theory', nor is it a prescription for a universal panacea. Rather it shares successful methods of enabling people to meet the needs of the times.

We believe the approach makes a – if not **THE** – significant difference in creating success through people, which for many organisations is the only, or most, significant potential competitive advantage they have.

**We hope it helps you, your organisation, your people.**

*GOOD LUCK*

## Chapter Summary

- *The approach to Leading & Developing High Performance described here is based on practical research into what effective practitioners actually do to bring about sustained High Performance.*
- *Such people are Leader/Developers – not just managers – what they do causes High Performance to happen.*
- *Leading & Developing High Performance is not a sweat-shop activity, but rather an approach founded on a mindset, a process and a set of competencies, which benefit all the stakeholders.*
- *The approach is readily available and can be learned by all; it does not need charismatic heroes to fulfil it. It does require, however, a set of competencies which are presently not widely taught.*
- *The High Performance Competencies are particularly important in the organisational context of today, where change has had a major impact on the way of working. They also equip Leader/Developers to cope well with inevitable, further change.*

# chapter 2

# Underlying Attitudes and Beliefs for Success

- *The Attitudes and Beliefs of Effective Leader/Developers*
- *The Mindset of High Challenge-High Support*
- *Challenge and Support Options: Choices and Consequences*
- *Organisation Culture, Change and High Challenge-High Support*
- *Knowing your Challenge-Support Profile*
- *Rights and Responsibilities of Leader/Developers*
- *Rights and Responsibilities of Team Members*
- *Reinforcing Concepts and Attitudes:*
  - *Expectations Theory*
  - *Reinforcement Theory*
  - *Positive Regard and Genuineness*
- *Another Useful Perspective – The OK Corral*
- *Chapter Summary*

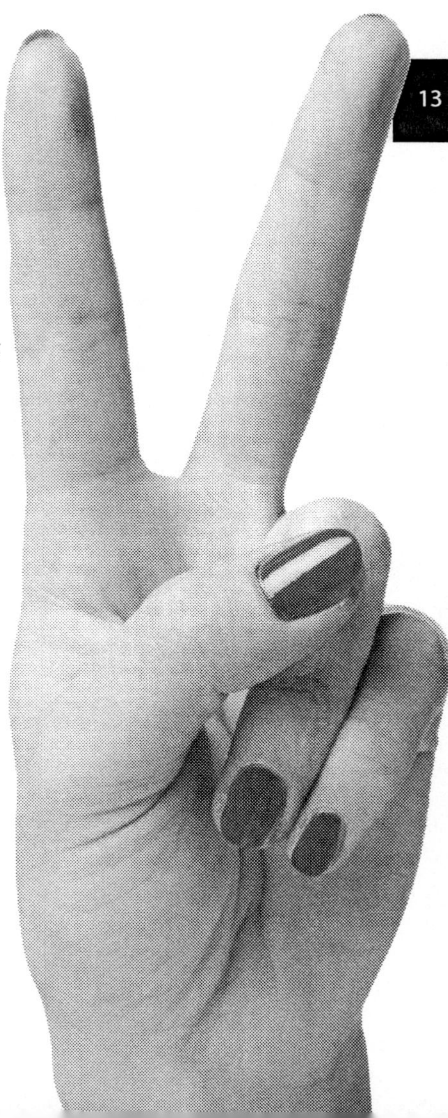

# The Attitudes and Beliefs of Effective Leader/Developers

Successful Leader/Developers of High Performance in today's world share, above all, one thing in common. This emerged strongly from our research. What they had in common was their Underlying Attitudes and Beliefs, held consistently by those Leader/Developers who achieved sustained high performance. Such people do not walk around with a placard around their necks proclaiming what they believe in, rather they act them out, live them, breathe them, demonstrate them. When we discussed performance development with such people it was clear that the Beliefs were very strongly held; it was as though they were permeated with them, just as a stick of rock carries its signature throughout its entire length. They were rock-like too in the way they held onto these beliefs, even when encountering difficulty and resistance, including those occasions when they were not entirely successful.

The way we see people and situations, the particular 'lens' we use, defines them for us and strongly influences the way we react and behave. Some people may see a glass half empty while another will see it half full. While one person may see another as worthwhile, competent and with something to offer, another person's 'lens' will see that same person as 'not to be trusted', 'out to get me' or incapable and needing to be looked after.

Sometimes, in modern management speak, this 'lens' is called a *paradigm*.

We prefer to call it Underlying Attitudes and Beliefs, or simply a *Mindset*. Whatever it is called, the way we respond to a situation, what we say and do, the action we take and the way we carry it out, will all flow from it. It is the 'mainspring' of the way we relate to and deal with people. Covey, in his book '*The Seven Habits of Effective People*', gives a very good example of this:

> *The scene is the New York subway early on a Sunday morning. All is quiet and peaceful as the train waits to depart; the passengers are reading their Sunday newspapers or enjoying a moment of quiet reflection. Then onto the train comes a man with some children. The children proceed to run up and down the corridors, pulling at newspapers and creating much noise and disturbance. The man (the father) just sits slumped in a seat, not interfering with what is going on.*

*Eventually Covey approaches the father intending to remonstrate with him to resolve the problem. (We can readily imagine Covey's feelings and the way he was seeing the situation at this stage.) After some discussion, the father says "I'm sorry, I've just come from the hospital, my wife has just died, I don't know how I am going to cope and my children don't either."*

*Immediately the same situation is seen through a different 'lens' or paradigm. Covey's immediate response to the news is to want to help, to support. Any punitive thoughts and bad feelings have fled, he is seeing the same situation differently though a new 'lens' or paradigm.*



The most important characteristics for Leading and Developing High Performance in others is the Mindset, or Attitudes and Beliefs, you have concerning your people. Without these Attitudes and Beliefs you are unlikely to develop high performance in others. They underpin the skills required, and without them, the skills, no matter how perfectly honed, are unlikely to be effective. In fact the reverse is true; if you operate consistently from the right Attitudes and Beliefs you can achieve significant results, even though your skills may not be completely perfect. Attitude is all.

## ATTITUDE

*The longer I live, the more I realise the impact of attitude on life. Attitude, to me, is more important than facts. It is more important than the past, than education, than money, than circumstances, than failures, than successes, than what other people think or say or do. It is more important than appearance, giftedness or skill. It will make or break a company ... a church ... a home.*

*The remarkable thing is, we have a choice every day regarding the attitude we will embrace for that day. We cannot change our past ... we cannot change the inevitable. The only thing we can do is play on the one string we have, and that is our attitude ... I am convinced that life is 10% what happens to me and 90% how I react to it.*

**And so it is with you ... we are in charge of our Attitude**

# The Mindset of High Challenge-High Support

We call this set of Attitudes and Beliefs *High Challenge-High Support.* It is the deeply held and actioned frame of reference out of which Leader/Developers, who are mobilizers of human energy, act. Leading and Developing High Performance matters to these people; they do not simply go through the motions but instead invest of themselves in the process with passion, intensity and belief. Hence the term *High Challenge-High Support. Challenge* in the sense that they have high standards and expectations about what can be achieved, *Support* in the sense that they care about their people's success and put themselves out to bring it about.

*High Challenge-High Support* is not ***either/or*** it is ***both/and***. The concept challenges Leader/Developers to hold the two opposites in powerful and equal balance. Such Leader/Developers are, for example, prepared to push hard for increased quality of performance – even at the cost perhaps of losing some immediate popularity – and at the same time consistently give strong support and encouragement. They will deal with an emerging bad practice immediately, knowing that firm, early action will prevent a more developed situation from occurring which will cause more 'pain' to everyone to put right. They will trust people, but if anyone abuses that trust they will deal with them in no uncertain terms. They will both 'push' and 'pull' people through change, providing firmness of direction when necessary and the security of belief to people that they have the capability to win through. They will be direct and explicit in telling someone that a piece of work is not to the standard required and what is expected, and at the same time put themselves out to make sure the person succeeds. They are Developers, providing the impetus for people to stretch their boundaries and grow their capabilities, and the means through coaching and mentoring to do so. They are generous and tough enough to entrust people to use initiative, and at the same time to field genuine mistakes, treating such mistakes as an opportunity to learn and improve.



In previous years the style of management could be broadly described as a 'push' one, but exercised in a command and control fashion; this was eventually seen as not very productive and having many negative consequences. So the conventional wisdom became to swing the pendulum in the opposite direction, to a 'pull' one, concentrating on encouragement, participation and counselling based approaches.

In terms of McGreggor's Theory X and Theory Y management styles[a], there has generally been a polarisation towards Y, but it seems both babies were thrown out with the bath water. However, McGreggor was often misinterpreted; it is not the either/or of X and Y, but the **both/and** of Z, the ingredients of *High Challenge-High Support.* Another ingredient of *High Challenge-High Support* is the passion and intensity with which it is held. It is the **both/and** approach which so many Leader/Developers, when they come in contact with the concept, find so reassuring and 'grounding' as it fits with what they often intuitively feel is right.

*Support* is a strong term. Harrison gives a good description of Support when he talks about creating high levels of service in the workplace – "this involves looking for – and acknowledging – the good and positive in people, listening to their hopes and fears, seeing them as valuable and unique, responding to their needs and nurturing their growth". But Support by itself can be lopsided, if, as one Chief Executive put it, when pointing out the risks both to the business and the long term security of people, a 'soft, fool's paradise' approach is taken.



> *"People, of course, are far and away the most important resource in any company. But they are more than that. It is very easy to forget, when endeavouring to develop people and to care for them, and even to love them, that the needs of the business must come first. Without that, there can be no lasting security. A fool's paradise in which effort is concentrated only on the present well-being of the staff, without regard for the future, will eventually disintegrate and it may well be the staff that suffer most."*
>
> Management for the Future – Ashridge

An alternative way of looking at this point is:

> *"When the horses come to the forge it's the sentimental people who are the most trouble - so careful to be gentle that they forget to be firm; the horses get confused; they don't know what they're supposed to do and they get nervous and restless, it's just as hurtful as being too rough."*
>
> The Blacksmith – Jeremy Maxwell –Warner Books

[a] Theory X: People must be closely directed and controlled if they are to produce to standard

Theory Y: 'Participative' management will of itself bring out people's natural abilities and motivation to do well

What we are talking about is **both/and**, that is both High Challenge and High Support used in powerful and equal combination.

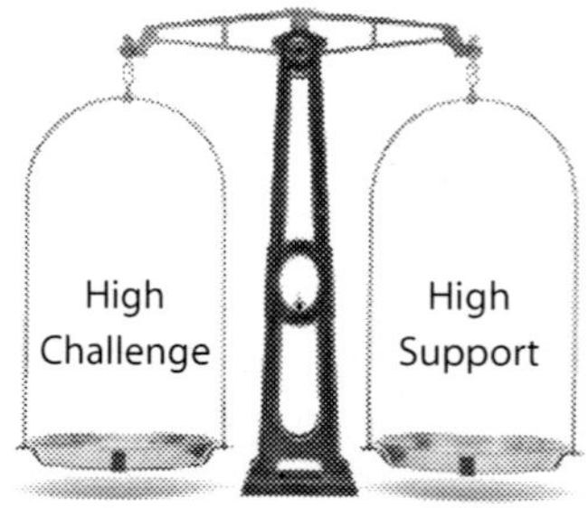




The same Chief Executive described this well.

> *"The needs of our business will be most effectively attained if the needs of people for fulfilment, success, and meaning, are met. If people are in poor shape, the company's objectives are unlikely to be achieved. Yet the needs of the business still come first. People need to be developed, but this will not be achieved by treating them with 'soft care', by allowing issues to be smoothed over without being properly addressed. To treat people without care will cause them, and therefore the business, to diminish. Experience suggests that the needs of people and the business will be best met if we treat ourselves with 'tough love' (ie care which does not shy away from tough decisions.) This is very different from 'macho' management which basically does not involve care. Tough love requires courage. Respect for the individual does not mean pandering to the individual's weaknesses or even wishes. Involving people through tough love to secure both their development and good performance requires managers to take the initiative."*

Management for the Future – Ashridge

We prefer the concept of *High Challenge/High Support* to 'tough love' as it describes, more accurately, what those High Performance Leaders actually provide. Essentially, though, we are describing the same phenomenon, including the Leader/Developer causing things to happen – ie, taking the initiative.

# Challenge and Support Options: Choices and Consequences

If the emphasis placed on both Challenge and Support varies from low to high, then there are four possible mindsets or positions a Leader/Developer can operate from at a given time:

|  | |  |
|---|---|---|
| Low Challenge | – | Low Support |
| Low Challenge | – | High Support |
| High Challenge | – | Low Support |
| High Challenge | – | High Support |



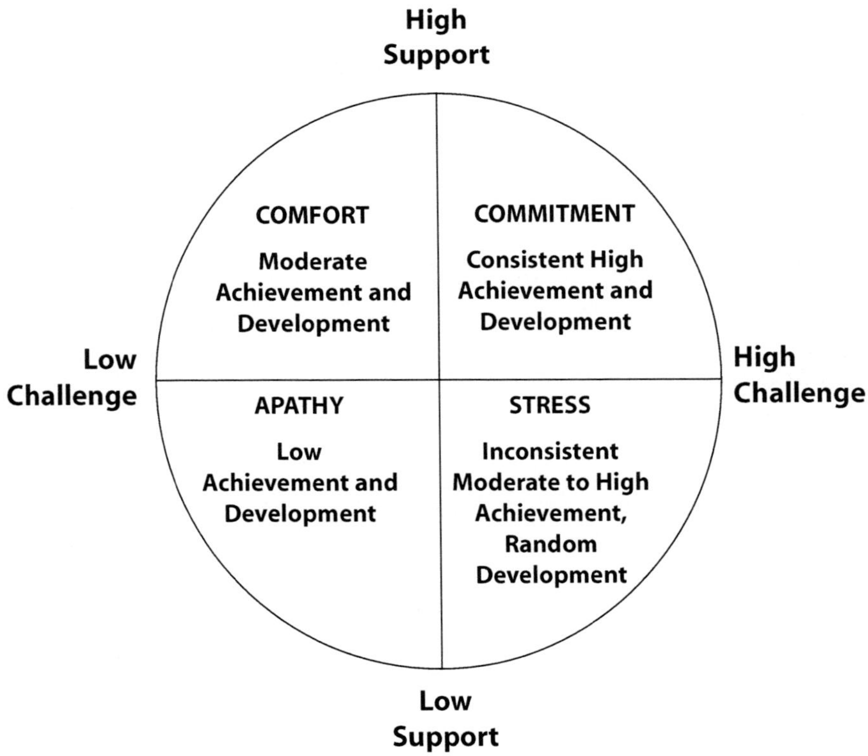

- ***Low Challenge – Low Support***

  *This results in Apathy, with low achievement and development. It is not a nice place to be; meaningless, nothing matters, no zest and fun, inward looking and riddled with 'jobs worth'. Those people who join teams led this way come to realise that energy and enthusiasm is misplaced, no one takes any notice if you do good work, and there is little comeback if performance and quality is low. Why bother? Nothing seems to matter!*

  *The Leader/Developer who operates this way, perhaps out of a misguided view of participation, or maybe because they feel a quiet life is what people want, is doing not only the organisation a disservice but, unfortunately, a major one to team members.*



  *The first rule of warfare is said to be to defend your home base – that is, for most of us, the security of employment or employability. Team members who are managed in this way, will lose their fitness to survive in today's world and will have an impoverished, unsatisfactory and poor quality working life.*

- ***Low Challenge – High Support***

  *This is the Comfort position, where the expectations placed on people are moderate, but where they are well 'looked after' both materially and with courtesy, concern and attention. It is frequently an approach taken by Paternalistic Organisations (often Benevolent ones) and at its heart is a Dependency view of people. Here the mindset is that people want to, or should, remain dependent on the greater expertise of others – typically their manager – rather than being more self-directing.*

  *In this position moderate achievement and development is likely to occur. However, difficulties happen when change is encountered, either when there is a requirement for more to meet increasing standards from competition, or when new ways of doing things are required. Such organisations and teams often have the greatest difficulty in breaking out of Comfort into doing new things, or the same things necessarily better, more so than even High Challenge–Low Support ones. Operating this way can indeed be to operate in a 'fool's paradise', as a hostage to fortune, with people not being 'the best they can be' but being complacently good enough for the present.*

- ***High Challenge – Low Support***

  *This is the Stress position, much experienced by many organisational members in this rapidly changing era. It is stressful because although a few people thrive on High Challenge without Support, the majority of us do not, particularly in times of change when new boundaries have to be crossed. It is the 'sink or swim' version of leadership.*

  *The problem with sinking or swimming is that some people don't ever learn to swim, and those who do often pick up faulty techniques. It is no wonder then that achievement is inconsistent, even though it can be moderate to high, and development is random because what is learned, if at all, is accidental. This is why, very often, attempts to make people 'empowered' have not altogether succeeded well. If Challenge is there without the Support enabling systems, such as reinforcement, encouragement, training etc, then such challenges are unlikely to be consistently and well met.*



- ***High Challenge – High Support***

  *This is the Commitment or leadership position where the Leader/Developer makes a difference by having both high expectations of what can be achieved, and actively enabling people to grow and develop to meet such challenges. It is particularly important during change because successful change does not happen by itself – it is led, consolidated and sustained.*

  *Such an approach equips team members to secure their own success, and to operate with responsible initiative and energy, rather than just being dependent. It is not a 'big bang' approach but instead is founded on continuous improvement, step by step, led by the Leader/Developer, until each team member takes on the approach themselves as a way of life.*

  *This is the approach best guaranteed to generate commitment to what needs to be achieved and to cause consistent high achievement and development. It was the one consistently applied by those Leader/Developers who led high performance teams.*

# Organisation Culture, Change and High Challenge – High Support

Yet another perspective is given by looking at Organisational Culture – the way things are done around here – which will be the most suitable for your organisation, department or team. A useful framework for exploring culture, describing four main types, and hybrids between them, is :

| | |
|---|---|
| **The Power Culture** | Authoritarian and hierarchical, dominated by 'strong' leader(s), with an emphasis on status and politics. |
| **The Role Culture** | Also hierarchical, but with power exercised through rules, systems and procedures, with an emphasis on predictability and correctness. In its extreme form a bureaucracy. |
| **The Achievement Culture** | 'Making a difference,' actioning a purpose or goal to which the individual is committed, taking appropriate action to achieve useful things. |
| **The Support Culture** | Motivation and bonding through close, warm relationships, trust and care, co-operation, responsiveness and belonging. |



The basic argument is that in today's fast moving, competitive world, cultures based on Power or Role are increasingly unsuitable for 'unlocked' service based and responsive organisations. They operate on an 'external' motivation or command and control principle. Instead what is required is an Achievement based culture, and this, broadly speaking, is the direction many organisations are taking with their various change programmes under the labels of empowerment, TQM, customer service, organisational effectiveness or whatever.

While working in an Achievement culture can provide opportunities for members to use their talents in ways which are more deeply satisfying, it can also make higher demands on its members' time and energy and, if unsupported, can lead to 'burn out'.

Also changing a culture from, say, a Role to an Achievement based one won't happen by itself, it needs Support. However, as has been said, a Support based culture by itself, although bringing necessary ingredients such as co-operation, responsiveness, caring, commitment to others (which connect, amongst other things, to high customer service), has in-built weaknesses. For example, tough decisions about people may be postponed, or consensus overvalued, so that timely decisions are not made, or inadequate performance is not challenged. So, we are looking at a culture based on Achievement and Support – High Challenge-High Support in fact.

The combination of the two, in powerful and equal balance, will also do much to alleviate the strain and stress that achievement and high performance can bring, when the focus is just High Challenge and High Achievement. With High Challenge-High Support, too, the motivation is 'internal' once the approach is established, rather than being externally driven and forced through, which brings about a different and more acceptable and sustainable relationship with the Challenge of the job.



There is one further factor to take into account, and this is the notion of Personal Power. A power source is needed to cause Achievement – nothing will happen without it – but it is a different kind of power than the one based on position and authority of the 'stripe on arm' variety. Rather, it is based on the Person and not the Position; it is what we call Personal Power.

> Today, success hinges on the ability to influence people to achieve common goals and purposes. This power to influence is personal effectiveness.
>
> It is the new power of competence. Such power is based on the person, not their position.
>
> It is ............ PERSONAL POWER

Personal Power is the energy and influence source which fuels the Leader/Developer's effective use of the *High Challenge – High Support* approach. It is not the position held, but what he or she does – what is believed, acted out and simply done. It is not the position but who is in the position which counts, their commitment and will to make a difference. Effective Leader/Developers define the situation for themselves, they are part of it, and if they use the 'lens' of the beliefs of *High Challenge – High Support* and demonstrate this consistently in practice, they will make that difference.

High performance in today's organisations requires increasingly the taking and acceptance of responsibility and initiative. This is one definition of that much overused word '*Empowerment*'.



Such enabled behaviour stems from power (Em**power**ment), and underpins achievement. This is power based on the person, personal power again, and the development of such personal power in team members will be one of the goals of the effective Leader/Developer.

# Knowing Your Challenge-Support Profile

The phrase *High Challenge – High Support* is used to describe and encapsulate the Underlying Attitudes and Beliefs which underpin Leading and Developing High Performance. These are the foundations on which the whole is firmly supported; without their enduring presence, any edifice of skills will crumble and be experienced as just an edifice. You may not like the term *High Challenge – High Support*, no matter, choose your own, what really matters is whether you adapt the principles and beliefs as a way of leading others, and as the springboard for developing high performance with each and everyone of your people.

At this stage, what is important is to review your current set of Underlying Attitudes and Beliefs in comparison with those Leader/Developers who have demonstrably secured high performance. Reviewing your Attitudes and Beliefs in this way will enable you to reposition yourself, if necessary, if you choose to do so, and will also help in focusing your own development.



It is likely that at present you will tend to incline either to the Support side or Challenge side; relatively few people, initially at least, are perfectly balanced in that they use both *High Challenge* and *High Support*, powerfully and equally. In subsequent chapters we will be dealing with the skills and processes necessary to promote high performance, and you will be able to review your relative strengths and weaknesses in such skills. Knowing whether you have a present tendency towards Support and therefore the skills involved with this, or vice versa, will also help you with your own development plan.

A way of summarising these Attitudes and Beliefs follows.

## Underlying Attitudes and Beliefs



Look at the following points, then check against the guide on the following page to see whether they incline more towards Challenge or Support.

**1. All the people I work with**
a) are basically OK people
b) have the ability to develop and change

**2. As the Leader I have the responsibility to create**
a) a clear vision and direction for the team
b) a high performing team

**3. People must be treated with**
a) courtesy and respect
b) the firm belief and expectation that they can perform highly and successfully adapt to change

**4. Communication must be**
a) frank, genuine and not manipulative

**5. As the Leader I have the right to**
a) be direct in telling people what I expect from them and to tell them when they are not delivering
b) demand the same level of courtesy and frankness that I give

**6. My overall aim is to**
a) help everyone who works with me to be the best they can be and thus feel good about their contribution and competence
b) achieve my vision of the team performing at its very best

**7. In order to achieve my aim I am prepared to**
a) sacrifice immediate popularity to push people to realise their full abilities
b) give them all the help and support I can to enable them to succeed

**8. People who fundamentally disagree with my overall aim**
a) have the right to do their own thing, elsewhere, and to go with my goodwill

You will notice that:

| | |
|---|---|
| 1a)<br>1b)<br>3a)<br>4a)<br>6a)<br>7b) | incline to *SUPPORT* |
| 2a)<br>2b)<br>3b)<br>5a)<br>5b)<br>6b)<br>7a)<br>8a) | incline to *CHALLENGE* |

You will be able to make a judgement about the direction of your own views. Remember, though, that it is the combination of *Challenge* and *Support* (the **both/and** principle) which really matters.

Another way of looking at the same Attitudes and Beliefs is to think about your Rights and Responsibilities as a Leader/Developer, and those of the people who work with and for you.

# Rights and Responsibilities of Leader/Developers

As a Leader/Developer, I have both Rights and Responsibilities. Equally, the people who work with and for me have Rights and corresponding Responsibilities.

My **RESPONSIBILITIES** include:

- *Creating a High Performance Team – one which is capable of delivering what will need to be done tomorrow as well as today*
- *Providing a clear sense of direction – to the department I lead*
- *Enabling people to achieve their full capability – even though this might not be immediately popular*
- *Being genuine – saying what I mean and meaning what I say and treating others with respect and frankness*
- *Giving of myself and my support – to enable the people in my team to succeed and being delighted when they do*
- *Letting people know how they are performing – continually, through strong feedback*
- *Causing people to stay 'fit for life' – for their sakes as well as mine in today's competitive world*



My **RIGHTS** include:

- *Demanding the same level of courtesy and frankness that I give*
- *Telling people what is expected of them, clearly and explicitly*
- *Letting them know when they are not performing through direct unambiguous feedback*
- *Setting the vision for the team and to drive for its attainment.*

This means adopting and living by the principle of

***High Challenge – High Support***

# Rights and Responsibilities of Team Members

Equally, Team Members have RIGHTS, which include:

- *Being treated with courtesy and respect*
- *For there to be a clear sense of direction – including knowing what is expected of them and the standard required*
- *Not following my vision, if they cannot agree with it – but to follow their own vision elsewhere*
- *Being regarded as a fundamentally OK person – who has the inherent ability to succeed and perform highly*
- *Knowing how they are getting on – regularly*



But with the RIGHTS go RESPONSIBILITIES, including:

- *Respecting the rights of the Leader/Developer*
- *Treating the Leader/Developer with courtesy and respect, equal to that given*
- *Performing highly and meeting the standards expected of them*
- *Continuously striving to learn, to grow and to improve their capability*
- *Doing all they can to enable the team, as a whole, to succeed*

> *This means that as the Leader/Developer I have to apply the principle of*
>
> ***High Challenge – High Support***
>
> *to myself as well as my team*

# Reinforcing Concepts and Attitudes

As well as holding firmly to and practising the underlying Attitudes and Beliefs of High Challenge-High Support, the effective Leader/Developers of High Performance we worked with, also operated to two crucial concepts which pervaded what they did. There were, in addition, two attitudinal characteristics which were important to them. Although they did not see them as an established theoretical underpinning for what they did, they are, in fact, just that.

| | |
|---|---|
| The *CONCEPTS*: | ▪ ***Expectations Theory***<br>▪ ***Reinforcement Theory*** |
| The *ATTITUDES*: | ▪ ***Positive Regard***<br>▪ ***Genuineness*** |



- ***Expectations Theory***

  *Expectations Theory is basically very simple. If expectations are high you tend to get more. If expectations are low you tend to get low or moderate performance. Effective Leader/Developers of High Performance always have high expectations about their people's performance and ability to develop and change, and work on this basis. It is a classic case of 'you get what you give'.*

  *Having low expectations on someone is like putting a curse on the person; it inhibits them from getting in touch with their real abilities, confidence and competence. It often confirms their own low self-esteem or view of the world. It reinforces, negatively – it is disempowering. Leader/Developers who operate from High Support without corresponding High Challenge, often cause others to remain dependent on them rather than causing them to grow their own competence and capability.*

The reverse is equally true. This is not to say that everyone is capable of becoming a brain surgeon. We are not talking about driving people beyond their capabilities but, equally, their potential capabilities are likely to be larger than they, and possibly you, presently think. Small victories and successes themselves change people's own expectations, raising the possibility and expectations of further successes; that success is possible and is the norm. This is reinforcing to positive self esteem which, in turn, leads to more growth and success.

The effective Leader/Developers of High Performance we encountered all had high expectations about what their people were capable of – and it mattered and it showed.

Expectations, high or low, are rather like body language in that they leak and people will pick up the signals and know how to respond. Also, your expectations will affect the way you approach, deal with and interact with people, generating effects of their own. Many scientific experiments have confirmed this with remarkable consistency.

> *Instructors at a Welding School were told that the brightest group of trainees were the least able, and vice versa. The group which was the less able but who the instructors believed were the most able achieved the best results.*



What seems to be the case, as a general rule, is...

- *You get what you give*
- *If you're prepared to be disappointed then you won't be disappointed*

The effective Leader/Developers were not naive about this, but they held it as an important principle. They also had the sense to see that to get to the end result they had in mind, they had to proceed in stages by working to a process of continuous improvement. The complementary theory to Expectations is Expectancy, and basically this says that people will come to a decision as to whether the outcome required is worth the effort they would need to put in, or the reward they would get; or whether the difficulty and effort was too great, and the reward too low for the value of the outcome as they saw it. In starting the process of Developing High Performance, based on High Expectations, 'chunking up' the whole into more digestible stages, is likely to be most successful, particularly if each step achieved is reinforced. It can also, very often, develop a momentum of its own.

There is, too, one other important aspect to High Expectations. This concerns the context of the workplace, simple but important standards like timekeeping, safety, the working environment etc. To put it crudely, if your expectations about these are low, or allowed to slip, then it is unrealistic to expect people to buy into the notion of High Performance.

For these things are exemplars and, moreover, poor standards with such basic functions will diminish what you are trying to achieve with everyone performing at their very best. It is similar to the so called 'broken window' phenomenon, where it is known that if a broken window is not attended to then there is a much greater risk of the building being vandalised than in the case where the window is repaired immediately and standards maintained. So it is with your expectations of High Performance; the broken window theory holds good here.

- ***Reinforcement Theory***

  *One other thing the effective Leaders/Developers had was a strong intuitive feel for the Reinforcement principle. In practice this means catching people doing something right, instead of only paying attention when things went wrong. They operated this way, again as a way of life, not just once a year at a formal appraisal review, but hour by hour, day by day, week by week. They looked out for improvements and reinforced them by strong positive feedback, encouraging people to do more of the same, as a way of continuously developing competence in small but important steps. At the same time they were prepared to, and gave, negative feedback when necessary as part of the whole. In both cases they used a subtle blend of rewards, and penalties or consequences, largely coming from themselves.*

*This is no mere Pavlovian 'stimulus-response' type conditioning. True, in the earlier stages of the process, stimulus of various kinds may be needed to get the response of a particular behaviour, and that behaviour may need to be reinforced. But the aim of these effective Leaders/Developers was to get the person to learn, releasing the person's own creativity, in a way where the learning becomes a self motivated activity. When this happens, the motivation source becomes not the 'push' one of externally applied rewards or punishments, but the 'pull' one which comes from the 'internal' motivation of the person themselves.*

*Again, this comes back to the attitude of the Leader/Developer as well as their skills. For one thing, effective ones are prepared to invest the effort and persistence. They see their people not as an accident about to happen, but as a great achievement about to unfold. One team member expressed it all very succinctly when commenting on his team leader.*



> *"He spoke to me as an equal, kicked my ass when I'd done something wrong, praised me when I did something right He was very good at communicating what was wanted and in keeping me involved. I thought I was important and I responded. I knew what was expected of me and I felt part of a team. It was down to me and I felt guilty if I didn't get the result."*

- ***Positive Regard and Genuineness***

  *Highly effective Leader/Developers of High Performance share two characteristics in common with effective counsellors. Research shows that effective counsellors need to have these two characteristics before they can help their clients and, if they don't display these characteristics, then their clients won't respond to them. These findings are extremely relevant to the way in which you discuss with someone their job performance, and help them to improve.*

The two characteristics are:

> *POSITIVE REGARD*
>
> *Which means having respect for the other person as an individual and a positive belief in them as a person.*

> *GENUINENESS*
>
> *Which means you are able to express your own feelings and tell the truth about your reactions to the other person's behaviour. It means being direct, open and honest with the other person.*

Without these underlying characteristics – again mostly attitudes – you are unlikely to cause the other person to change and enhance their performance. Also, without them, the interaction is likely to be experienced as false, patronising or manipulative. With them, however, not only is the process destined to go well, but the interaction does not have to be technically perfect in order to be successful.

In other words:

- *The underlying attitudes of Positive Regard and Genuineness, which are part of High Challenge-High Support, are even more important than the skills of conducting the discussion.*
- *Without them you will have little real influence on other people, particularly those whose performance you wish to help to improve significantly.*

Again, this is common sense. It is better to engage with the other person directly, as a human being, and not hide behind the façade of being always measured and dispassionate. It is about being straight with the other person, while valuing them as an individual.

Clearly this does not mean losing your temper or over-reacting. Rather, it is concerned with having sufficient Positive Regard for the other person to 'tell it like it is', concentrating on what they do (the behaviour) that is causing good or poor performance. It is the part of Positive Regard which values the person, but not necessarily their behaviour.

If you keep your feelings bottled up, they will leak out anyway through body language and may be misinterpreted. Alternatively, they will come out at a later stage with irritation or anger. Also, if the interaction is not open and honest – or worse still, is manipulative – then the other person will soon sense this. You can rarely keep feelings as hidden as you think you can !

Genuineness is part of Positive Regard and it is not possible to maintain Positive Regard without being Genuine. Both are essential for Leading and Developing High Performance.

## Another Useful Perspective – The OK Corral

The OK Corral is derived from Transactional Analysis, which is a way of looking at relationships between people. It describes a set of fundamental attitudes and beliefs which affect the way we see and respond to others.

From an early age, people develop a view of their own worth and tend to take 'Life Positions' relative to other people. Life Positions develop from experiences, particularly those during childhood, and affect the way people feel, act and relate.

The OK Corral Model is concerned with two basic views which you will operate to, perhaps subconsciously, when dealing with another person.



Firstly how you view yourself :

| | |
|---|---|
| ***I'm OK*** | My self esteem is reasonably high; I feel comfortable with this environment; I feel able to cope, etc... |
| ***I'm not OK*** | I'm uncomfortable dealing with this sort of issue; I don't feel I have the necessary skills etc... |

Secondly, how you view the other person:

| | |
|---|---|
| ***You're OK*** | You have a right to your opinions; you are essentially decent; you have a contribution to make, etc... |
| ***You're not OK*** | You never listen you are wrong; you won't win this one, etc... |

The combination of your view of yourself and your view of the other person, gives the possibility of four positions, or attitudes. Each position is typified by particular types of behaviour.

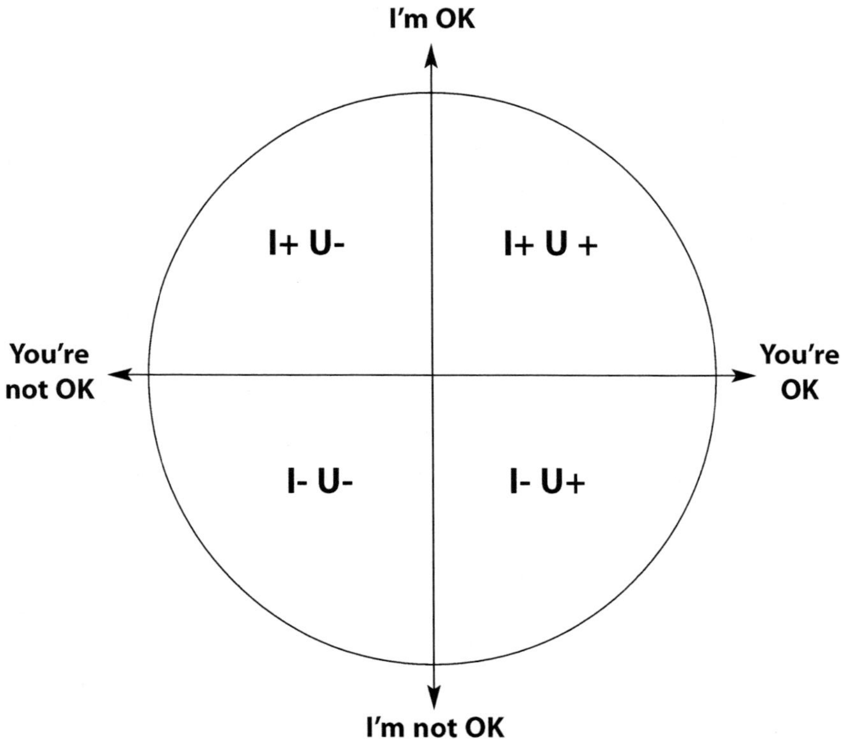

Descriptions of OK Corral Quadrants

I+ U- If this is your underlying attitude then your behaviour will indicate a feeling of superiority, either through an aggressive stance or alternatively an over-protective approach. This is likely to provoke resistance, aggressiveness or dependence from the other party. It is either a High Challenge-Low Support or Low Challenge-High Support one.

I- U- This attitude manifests itself in a suspicious and often hostile approach to others, with an underlying feeling of "Why bother – it won't make any difference anyway." To be on the receiving end of this type of behaviour can be frustrating and exhausting, and it requires considerable effort to deal with it appropriately. It is the Low Challenge-Low Support approach.

I- U+ If you're viewing life from this position on the OK Corral, it is likely that your self-esteem has taken a knock; you are strongly influenced by the other person, who is OK in your mind. Behaviours emanating from here are dependent, non-assertive and often yielding, which in turn can lead to a further dip in your self-esteem. It is another Low Challenge-High Support position. An interesting factor about those who often inhabit this quadrant is the lightning switch they can make to I+U-. When the final straw is delivered, the method of dealing with it is often an extremely aggressive approach which surprises all parties.

I+ U+ This is the most productive position to occupy, whenever possible. Behaviours are assertive but warm, and the underlying attitude is one of Positive Regard and trust, even when delivering bad news or a potentially unpleasant message. Your expectations of the other person are consistently high. When expectations are high, and supported by Positive Regard and Genuine behaviour, the chances of those expectations being met are significantly increased. This is the High Challenge-High Support position.

Effective Leaders/Developers operate from the I+U+ position, consistently, even at times of difficulty, and when dealing with poor performers whose position in the OK Corral is I-U+, I+U- or, most difficult of all, I-U-. There are a number of powerful reasons for this.

- *Being on the receiving end of I+U- behaviour promotes Dependency or Counter Dependency and Rebellion*
- *Being on the receiving end of I-U- behaviour promotes Withdrawal and Alienation*
- *Being on the receiving end of I-U+ behaviour promotes Dependency and Acquiescence*
- *Being on the receiving end of I+U+ behaviour promotes Independence and Interdependence*

Enabling someone to be the ***best they can be*** and performing at ***their very best*** means them not acting Dependently or rebelling against you and the organisation with Counter Dependence, but having themselves the attitudes, abilities, skills, confidence and competence to manage tasks Independently and, better still, Interdependently...

***...this is the mission for the Leader/Developer.***

# Chapter Summary

### Successful Leaders/Developers

- *Hold a strong set of Attitudes and Beliefs which they work to, consistently and in a way which is clearly visible to others.*
- *Operate to High Challenge* ***and*** *High Support, used in powerful and equal combination. It is not* ***either/or*** *but* ***both/and****.*
- *Recognise that the four combinations of Challenge and Support create differing outcomes, and they make a realistic conscious choice about what mindset to operate from.*
- *Understand the context and culture they are working in and use their own Personal Power to promote necessary change through a High Challenge-High Support approach, developing not only team members' skills and abilities, but also their Personal Power.*
- *Know their own bias to Challenge or Support, take this into account, and seek to develop their approach so that they are both used, consistently, in powerful and equal balance.*
- *Have a clear view of the Rights and Responsibilities of themselves as the Leader/Developer and also of those who work with them.*
- *Have high expectations of their people and what they can achieve. At the same time they work to a cumulative series of attainable goals, taking a step by step approach, but keeping their overall goal of enabling the team and its members to become the best they can be.*
- *Reinforce desired behaviours by catching people doing something right, when they make an improvement or take a step in the right direction. They also face up to and deal with negative feedback, to help people improve. They work in such a way that once people are moving in the right direction they will be self motivated to continue and learn.*
- *Have Positive Regard for others, which means having respect for them as an individual and a positive belief in them as a person.*
- *Are Genuine, in being direct, open and honest with the other person.*
- *Feel that they are OK and so is the other person (I+U+), and keep feeling this way even in times of difficulty – when they are able to see that it is not the other person who is not OK, but that person's behaviour.*
- *Do not want their people to remain or become Dependent on them, but see their role to enable people to develop not only their skills and knowledge, but their confidence, willpower and ability to manage tasks Independently/Interdependently.*

chapter 3

# What High Performance Leader/Developers Actually Do

- *The Four Step Process*
- *Process Skills and Behaviours Required*
- *Leadership or Management – What's the Difference?*
  - *Non-Leadership*
  - *Transactional Leadership*
  - *Transformational Leadership*
- *The Four Step Process Explored*
  - *Visioning Stage*
  - *Mobilising Stage*
  - *Developing Stage*
  - *Enabling Stage*
- *Competencies for Leading and Developing High Performance*
- *Chapter Summary*

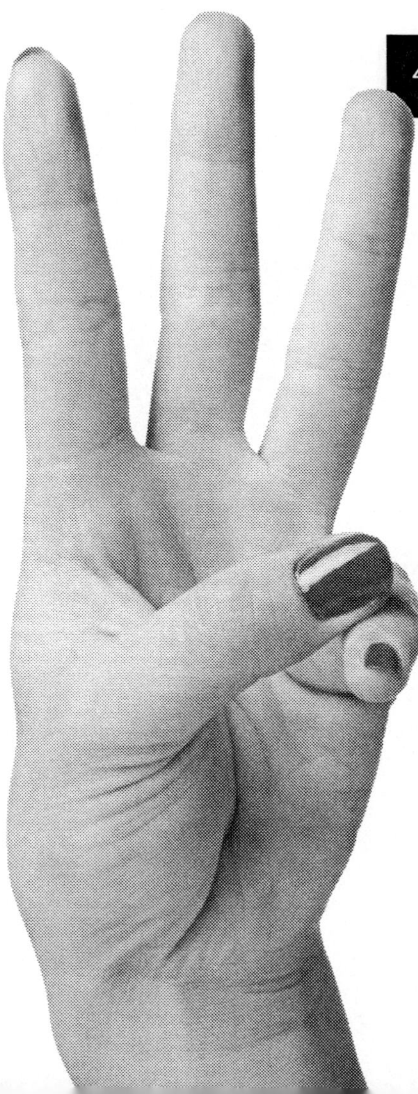

## The Four Step Process

What effective Leader/Developers actually do when maximising performance and people's potential is to follow a simple four step process. They work at the process constantly and with resolution. A number of skills are involved but, no matter how good their skills are, their application will not be truly effective unless used as part of a consistent process and with the right mindset. The process gives those leading others, and those new to such experience in particular, a 'track to run on' and a direction along which they can proceed with a sense of reassurance.

The process is basically a very simple four step one:



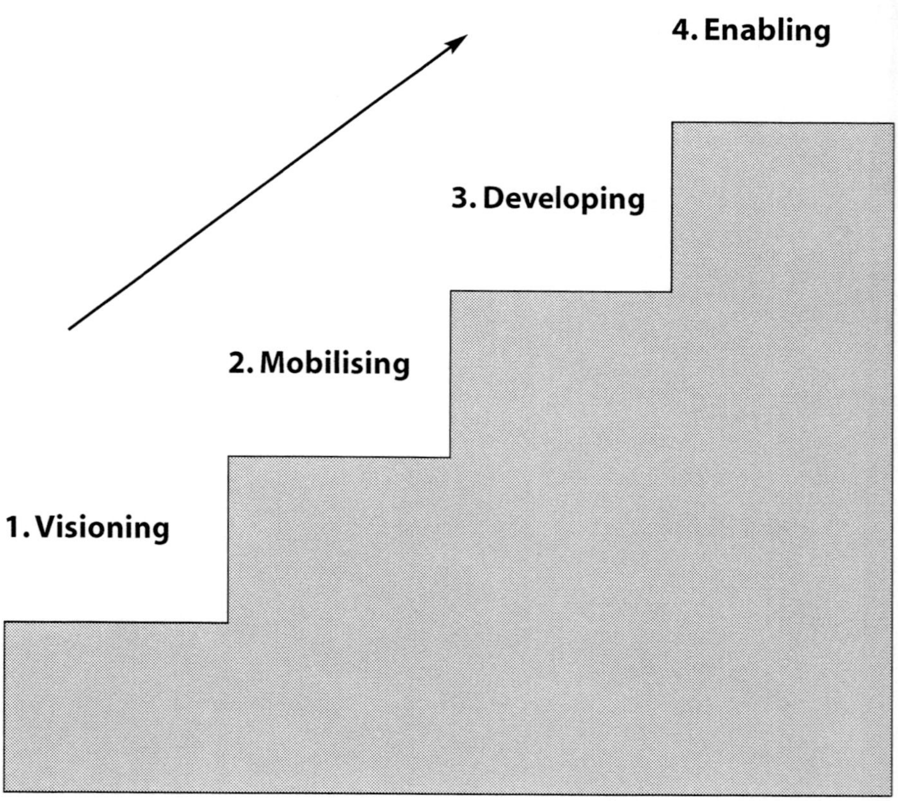

## Process Skills and Behaviours Required

| **1. VISIONING STAGE** | |
|---|---|
| Visibility of Personal Style | Projecting what you stand for, consistently |
| Observation and Information | Establishing facts and information about the present situation |
| Analysis | Analysing the present situation accurately |
| Vision | Creating a future vision of what needs to be done and the team performing at their very best |
| **2. MOBILISING STAGE** | |
| Clarity and Explicitness | Specifying what needs to be done for successful operation |
| Assertion | Being appropriately assertive and direct |
| Feedback | Giving strong, clear feedback in order to help people improve rapidly |
| Momentum | Resiliently maintaining direction and vision |
| Diagnosing Performance Issues | Diagnosing individual issues and their causes accurately |
| **3. DEVELOPING STAGE** | |
| Situational Consistency | Flexing style to match consistently team members' stages of development |
| Motivation | Being perceptive about individual strengths, needs and sources of motivation |
| Continuous improvement | Securing continuous improvement as a way of life |
| **4. ENABLING STAGE** | |
| Empowers | Actively building each team member's capability |
| Delegation | Investing trust through delegating task ownership |
| Continued Support | Maintaining support, encouragement and reinforcement |

These are described in more detail, and as a set of competencies, later in this chapter.

# Leadership or Management – What's the Difference ?

Before exploring the Four Step Process, it's useful to get clear the difference between leadership and management as it greatly affects the way the whole process is used and applied.

You will have noticed that we use 'leaders' rather than 'managers' when describing the developers of high performance. Those effective Leader/Developers of High Performance we encountered most certainly held a leadership view of their roles.

One of the differences between leadership and management is that Leader/Developers identify and action the direction to take, while managers are more concerned with carrying things out in good order. Imagine a group hacking its way through the jungle. The manager will be there, working very hard, making sure that the machetes are sharp, wiping sweat from fevered brows, looking after the well being of the workers, keeping morale high – all essential tasks. The leader, on the other hand, will, in addition, be the person who climbs up a tree to scout the way ahead. The leader is concerned with a future direction, not with just maintaining well the status quo. So it is with developing High Performance.



Another way of defining the difference is that 'managers do things right, Leader/Developers do right things'. Leader/Developers make a difference and add value. Change needs leadership; it doesn't happen by itself, at least not well, and much development is concerned with change, and change with development. Leader/Developers are part of the situation and define it. There are three levels of leadership:

- ***Non-Leadership***
  *'Leader/Developers' who avoid decisions, withdraw when needed, are uninvolved and take no stand*
- ***Transactional Leadership***
  *Leader/Developers who determine what their people need to do to achieve objectives, clarify those requirements, then help, and ensure, they become achieved*
- ***Transformational Leadership***
  *Leaders who, through their personal vision and energy, inspire their people and have a major input. Such leaders motivate people to achieve and develop much more than would be thought possible, and help connect them with the energy of their own internal motivation and needs*

Transactional Leaders tend to be primarily action orientated, whereas Transformational Leaders tend to have, and use, a higher degree of vision. 'Vision' is to do with creating images of future goals while 'Action' is to do with the execution of immediate behaviours. Both are necessary in Leading and Developing High Performance, the Transactional approach in the earlier stages of the process particularly, the Transformational approach to get people to realise their true potential and become the *best they can be*. It's a case of not **either/or** but **both/and**.

> *Vision without action is just a dream, and action without vision is meaningless and boring*



Not everyone is a charismatic Napoleon, Wellington, Churchill or Gandhi – thank goodness. We are not talking about charisma here, but a set of skills, underpinned by the mindset of *High Challenge-High Support*, applied within a process and carried out with Personal Power – rather than Positional Power.

It's now time to explore the Process and Skills in more detail. Assume you have been asked to take on a new group or department, so you will be looking at a situation afresh.

# The Four Step Process Explored

## 1. Visioning Stage

| V1: **Provides Consistency of Approach and Personal Style** | *Projecting and holding a clear personal style and a strong sense of who they are and what they stand for, which is clearly visible to others* |
|---|---|

Often the most challenging job is a person's first leadership one, no matter how junior in the organisation. This is particularly so if you are assuming leadership of a group of which you are already a member. The immediate issue is how you should relate to people in the group. This also applies, albeit to a lesser extent, to more experienced Leader/Developers.



At the one extreme there are those Leaders who position themselves to be aloof, hostile even, while at the other, some Leaders try to form buddy-buddy relationships with their team members. There are dangers involved in both these extremes. Being approachable and friendly without either trying to be 'one of the lads', or being remote, is usually the best choice to make. This enables you to both stay in contact with people and, at the same time, deal with any inappropriate behaviour, without being seen as two faced. Being Genuine and having Positive Regard for team members, is very much part of this.

**Relationship Style: Safety and Danger Zones**

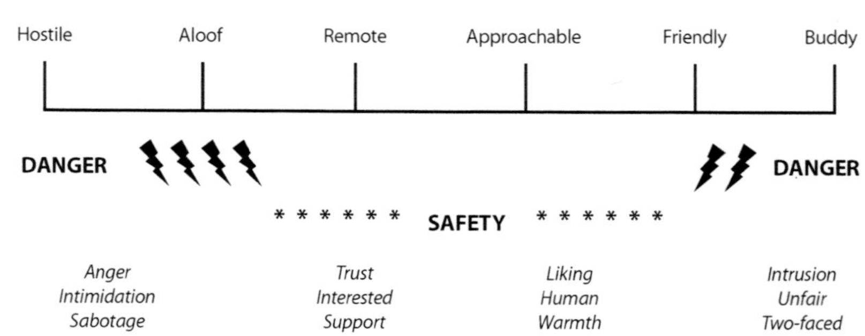

One of the fears that new Leader/Developers to a group are often concerned with is how they will be regarded by the group. *"Will I be liked by them?" "Will I be respected?" "Will they set out to give me a hard time?"* What is important in the situation is to have a clear set of personal standards, to live by them and make them visible to others. In almost all groups where a new leader is introduced, there is some testing out of the new leader to establish what the ground rules are, and test the boundaries.

It may involve only one person but the rest of the group will be watching. If the new leader does not deal with the situation in a way which is consistent to what they stand for, then, at its minimum, a lot of ground will be lost.



In this initial stage you are unlikely yet to have a distilled view about the future direction and what can be improved. If, however, you have and project a clear personal style and a strong sense of what you stand for, which is clearly visible to team members, then this is helpful to them. From the perspective of the team, if the new team leader is being enigmatic or guarded, this can add to the stress and uncertainty in what already may be a difficult situation for them. On the other hand, if it is clear what the leader stands for, and what is important to him or her – the 'rules of engagement' so to speak – people know where they are. It helps enormously if what you stand for is firmly routed in the beliefs of *High Challenge-High Support*.

What also matters is that such an approach is consistently carried out – it should not depend on what side of the bed you got out of that morning, or how you feel at the moment, or whether you personally like or dislike the person you are dealing with – so that people will catch on quickly that behaving in one way will get a response from you...

...and behaving in another way will produce a different response.

| V2: | Observation and Information | *Listening and questioning effectively to establish facts and information; consulting with others to get views; perceptively observing differences between what is said and done, and where improvements can be made* |
|---|---|---|

Leader/Developers make a difference and add value. So the first stage in the process is to see where improvements in performance can be made. This means reviewing present directions and levels of performance thoroughly and well, being careful to identify the 'good' as well as the 'less good', and not throwing the baby out with the bathwater.



In this stage there is a trap to avoid. The trap is in moving forward blindly, perhaps based on assumptions, without proper diagnosis of the situation. This is sometimes brought about by the 'John Wayne' syndrome, which is to do with the self image of the tough, gun slinging action man, who knows right from wrong, and who gets things 'sorted' right away.

Watch out too for the 'hero' syndrome where the expectations are (either self imposed or by the 'hero' boss), that miracles will be wrought in the first few days, if not hours. Then, too, there are those who have the solution (usually ready made) before understanding the problem – they leave a trail of ravaged, damaged groups, departments and even companies in their wake.

It is crucial to analyse the situation accurately, which requires data and information obtained not only from observation, but by good quality questioning and listening to others, including your own group. It is neither autocracy, nor is it weak consensus or compromise; at the end of the process it is the leader who will need to sift the information, come to conclusions and set out the path. This leads to:

| V3: | Analyses Present Situation Accurately | *Seeing above the waves; sifting information and forming views without jumping to conclusions; managing complexity without becoming submerged by it* |
|---|---|---|

It may be that performance in the team is uniformly high already, or it may be that it is a lot less than that. Whatever the situation, there is always a case for enhancing performance still further. In the case of already High Performers, as the saying goes, *"You don't have to be ill to get better.*" Whatever the situation now, once the analysis step is achieved, it's necessary to start visualising future possibilities, not just managing and monitoring the status quo of the present. Now is the time to create a clear, future sense of direction about what is to be done.

| V4: | Creates a Future Vision | *Developing a clear, future sense of direction about what is to be done, which adds value; creating that vision for self and transmitting enthusiasm for and commitment to it; visioning everyone in the team performing at their very best and being the best they can be* |
|---|---|---|



A Vision is the image we have of a desired future state. It is like stepping forward in time and seeing things as they will be. The Vision gives a future direction, which can be made to happen, rather than simply reacting to events, like a piece of driftwood in the undertow. It gives meaning and purpose to what we do.

Images are powerful and sometimes scary things. They set out the challenge we place on ourselves if we are to convert them to concrete reality. They also focus our energies on doing 'the right things' and can sustain our direction and persistence when things sometimes don't go smoothly and our resilience is gnawed at.

What effective Leader/Developers have in common is a strong, clear vision, generated by themselves and to which they are committed. This vision includes the task, business or technical developments but it is also strongly concerned with people – visioning the team and every member within it performing at their very best, being the best they can be, and using their full potential.

For they know that when it comes to achieving full effectiveness it is people who make the difference.

As one Chief Executive put it:

> *"Long term we have no sustainable competitive advantage in Capital Investment, Technology, Scale. Our real potential competitive differentiation could be our people and how effectively they contribute to the business."*

'People performing at their very best' is not just a Transactional view, but a Transformational one if people's capability and capacity are enlarged in a way that they become self actualising and internally motivated, working to Independence and Interdependence rather than just through command and control. This is the 'meta' vision Transformational Leader/Developers hold on to, believe in and action through their High Challenge-High Support approach. So, it is more than skills and knowledge that such Leader/Developers grow in others, but attitudes, self belief, confidence and self direction. They are 'empowerers'.

All this may sometimes seem difficult, if not impossible, to achieve, perhaps particularly so when compared with the reality of present performance levels. Visioning is also something that not everyone finds easy. One way to do it is to:

- *Let your mind project forward say one or two years into the future.*
- *Write down your vision of how your team will be performing at its very best. Describe in concrete, real terms what they will actually be doing and how you will know they are succeeding, for each individual. You don't need an essay, just a few statements.*
- *Now do this for the individual members of the team. Hang on to your belief that you can make a difference, even though you may currently have some poor or limited performers.*

The next step is to stay where you are in the future time, but look backwards to the present situation, visualising the journey between the two situations as a flight of steps. Imagine each team member climbing the steps to join you, at different speeds perhaps and starting from different positions, but coming to join you. You will know the step each person is starting from by virtue of the analysis of the current situation you have carried out, having identified the key ones and priority areas.

Achieving the vision means working to a series of (small) steps. It's like eating an elephant – it can only be done one mouthful at a time. The other realities are:

- *Nothing will change, certainly not in any focused, concerted way unless you cause and enable it to do so.*
- *If you don't have a vision, and thus a direction, any movement will be accidental and you could end up in the 'wrong' place, or just drift.*

This brings us back to Vision and Action again. Vision without action is just a dream; and action without vision is meaningless and boring. The action is in the purposeful doing, which we will shortly explore further when looking at the Mobilising Stage of the process.



It may be that your team are high performers already; highly skilled, capable and motivated. But this does not mean that they can stand still and, anyway, it will be doubtful if they are all 'perfect' in achieving professional mastery. The same principles apply; the difference is that your task is an easier one, but equally one with more responsibility, for by taking the soft option of pretending everything is perfect, or allowing the team to stand still or slip, is to do them an injustice. The level of ability, experience and commitment in the team may also be such that you will want to involve them more fully in the vision building, but it is the Leader/Developer who will need to make the final judgements as he or she is the person best positioned to do so.

You have a direction, a vision, which includes a picture in your mind's eye of each and every member of your team performing to their full potential. You may be seeing ordinary people doing extraordinary things, of which they don't know yet they are capable. You may be seeing a winning team operating in a new way, thriving on change, reaching new levels of competence. You may be visioning habitually dependent people, reluctant to change their ways, who become empowered, decisive and highly productive. You may be visioning already successful people achieving improved results with less stress and more enjoyment.

None of this is likely to happen by itself. It is the leader who can make the difference – not overnight, usually - but steadily, stage by stage, by consistently and patiently working to a process which involves key steps and priority areas. It is the leader, and the leader as developer and coach, who will make the crucial influence.

It is time too, to share that vision, that future perspective, with your team. You know where you and your group are going and it's time to start the journey. Knowing where you are going, keeping the goal firmly in mind, being clear about what you want to achieve with and for your team, will enable you to maintain direction, as well as meet and overcome the difficulties which will inevitably occur.

## 2. Mobilising Stage



The Mobilising Stage comes before the Developing one. 'Developing' means increasing participation. But, there is example after example of groups with new Leaders, or those reformed or reorganised through change, not altering the way they operate and having diffuse and varying goals. To move straight into high participation as a basis for development, without having first established and reinforced the direction and the standards required, is to promote misunderstanding and future difficulty.

Like '*motherhood*' and '*apple pie*', participation is regarded as a 'good thing' – it is – but in terms of its effectiveness the ground has to be prepared first. We are not talking about heavy handed or repressive 'Leadership' here (on the contrary it's light but firm, and enabling), or a return to the old command and control methods, what we are talking about rather is an approach which has both high expectations of people's capability to contribute excellently, coupled with high support to enable them to achieve that contribution.

The problem can be that the team may have become complacent, or individual members have done it 'this way' for the last 700 years, or they may be comfortable in the security of the known, or they are not ambitious about their own performance capability. To disturb the status quo may often not be popular at first, or generate resistance, and this is where holding on to the principles of *High Challenge-High Support* becomes particularly important. Sometimes a new Leader will find that the group is already functioning well, with a clear and uniform sense of direction which only needs fine tuning, and operating to a level of ability and commitment which is exceedingly high. In such cases, the Leader's task is made easy, or more difficult – for if a change in direction is required, it will be like turning the proverbial oil tanker.

The Mobilising Stage is about establishing the future direction, standards required, way of operating and aligning and connecting people to the vision, so they become committed to it. It may involve breaking present habits. It is very different from everyone being loosely bound together but doing their own thing and working to their own agendas. The Mobilising Stage is rather like the experiment with iron filings we experienced at school, with the direction of the particles being random, until a magnet was drawn over them and they all pointed in the same direction, creating their own magnetic pull.

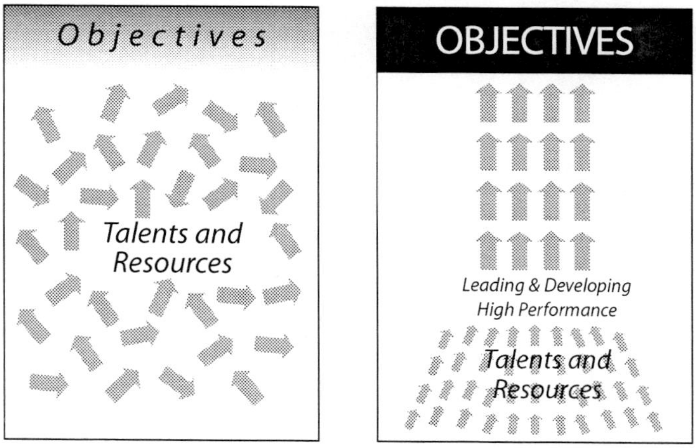


In this Mobilising Stage the Leader/Developer gets people 'on side', wanting to improve, taking increased ownership and responsibility for what they do, doing what is right - within the context of the vision. The competencies required are as follows:

| M1: | Provides Clarity and Explicitness | *Specifying in clear, unambiguous behavioural terms, what is required for successful operation, and what will be regarded as poor performance* |
|---|---|---|

A skill much needed during the Mobilising Stage is that of being **explicit**, in clear behavioural terms, as to what is required. This is a much undervalued and underdeveloped skill, in the UK at least. Often the receiver has to guess what is required from him or her, messages are fuzzy and confused, what makes for successful performance is unclear, and obfuscated by a veneer of supposed politeness and courtesy. Being explicit is particularly important in situations of change, or where changes in behaviour are required.

Far from being patronising to the individual, as will be shown later, explicitness is helpful and empowering in enabling individuals to succeed, when it is carried out well and appropriately.

| M2: | Maintains Own Assertiveness | *Applying appropriately the underlying skills and attitudes of assertiveness, necessary for being explicit and giving feedback, but also to maintain consistency of standards and approach; exerting strong leadership, when necessary, to prevent the team going in different directions.* |
|---|---|---|

Assertiveness, as is well known, is not aggression, and certainly not passivity. It means respecting both your rights and those of the other person, staying in and operating from the I+U+ positions and stating clearly and directly what you require, without putting the other person 'down'. Assertiveness is often particularly important during the early stage of the process, and also for maintaining direction and standards, and for giving clear feedback.

| M3: | Gives Strong, Clear Feedback | *Giving feedback, both positive and negative, clearly and continuously to reinforce positive results and correct the negative ones, in order to help the person to improve rapidly* |
|---|---|---|

During this Mobilising Stage, especially, strong feedback is given clearly and continually to reinforce positive results and correct the negative ones, in order to help the person to improve rapidly. This is given as soon as appropriate, or inappropriate behaviour is seen, and not stored up for some later occasion. The principle is to **catch people doing something right**, thus reinforcing that behaviour, and likewise to let them know when they are not on track. What we are talking about here are not just major changes that are spotted, but also those small important ones which, if reinforced, will cumulatively make a major difference. We will be looking later, and in greater detail, at giving feedback well.

| M4: | Resiliently Retains Momentum and Direction | *Learns rapidly from events and experiences; is flexible in retaining overall vision; not thrown off course by setbacks and difficulties; keeps and resiliently pursues overall sense of direction* |
|---|---|---|

Many situations can be both rewarding and sometimes frustrating, where progress can be slow and then quick, where individuals can improve and then regress. It requires resilience to keep going, to retain direction and your overall vision, and not be thrown off course by setbacks and difficulties. Having and retaining a strong vision and sense of mission will be what will keep you on track to make consistent progress, as will maintaining your own assertiveness capacity.



| M5: | Diagnoses Performance Issues Accurately | *Accurately diagnosing the root cause of an individual's performance issue; identifying the issue in specific behavioural terms, and the underlying reasons, and deciding on a course of effective action to bring about the changes necessary* |
|---|---|---|

Yet another important skill for this stage is diagnosing performance issues accurately. This is not easy to do. However, unless we get an accurate fix on the root cause of the issue, we are unlikely to make much progress. Most of us are used to analysing problems in our own discipline, those concerning people tend to give us far more difficulty. Again, there is a process which helps considerably with explaining and diagnosing these issues, by looking at the difference between 'can't do' and 'won't do' and the underlying rewards or payoffs, or avoidance of consequences, people get when behaving as they do. People aren't daft – they do things for a reason, and understanding and dealing with these reasons is what matters.

## 3. The Developing Stage

Responses from individuals are likely to vary during the Mobilising Stage. Some may grasp the new direction very quickly and move to achieve it, whilst others resist and seem unable or reluctant to change. One individual will see what needs to be done and will do it well, while another may remain entirely dependent on you to be told what to do. Some may avidly want to acquire new skills and try them out, while other people can't see the point of doing so.

Also, if you are managing significant change, you will soon notice that some people adapt readily, while others need much more time. This doesn't mean that the slower people won't get there, it's likely to mean that it just needs more patience and effort. Seeing others who are through the 'boundary' and who are coping and thriving will provide role models.

When people are caught 'doing it right' consistently, it is time to reinforce and signal the process by flexing your style to provide more participation, involvement and shared decision making. This is the time to invite their views and suggestions, to move to a coaching and then mentoring style - as will be described in Chapter 9 – if progress is maintained. Your behaviour and approach to the team member should be consistent to what the individual does, and how he or she is performing. This is where **situational consistency** matters.

| D1: | Flexes Style Appropriately: Is Situationally Consistent | *Deals with individuals on the basis of what they do, not who they are; everyone knows clearly where they stand and that particular behaviours are responded to in consistent, particular ways; is able to flex style appropriately to deal with various levels of performance and commitment to overall vision* |
|---|---|---|

Participation and trust are important sources of reward, and give impetus for the individual's capability, self esteem and confidence to flower and grow.

With other people, where progress is slower, you may still need to apply close supervision and be explicit and directive in what is to be done and how. When such people make progress, you can then flex your style, treating everyone consistently according to what they do, not who they are, so that everyone knows clearly where they stand and that particular behaviours are responded to in consistent, particular ways. The process is one which builds capacity and develops performance continually. It is underpinned by knowing each member as an individual - their strengths and weaknesses, their motivation patterns and what matters to them.

| D2: | Knows Individual Needs and Motivations | *Relating to team members as individuals; realistic and knowledgeable about own and others' strengths and weaknesses; perceptive in knowing individuals' motivation patterns and needs, and skilled in providing appropriate rewards* |
|---|---|---|



The starting point here is to know your own motivation patterns and needs, for it is far too easy to assume, unthinkingly, that other people are the same as you and what matters to you will matter to them. People are the same in that they hold much in common, but different in that all are unique individuals, each with their own patterns of needs and wants. Knowing each individual as an individual will enable you to fine-tune your approach, within the context of situational consistency, so that you can connect with the person appropriately.

For example, one person may rejoice in increased responsibility (which is a reward to them), while another will want the security of not taking the risk (where they currently see responsibility as a penalty not a reward). One person may be eager for the achievement of personal mastery in the job, while another is 'just there for the money'. Yet another person may thrive on challenges, while someone else likes certainty and comfort.

Then again, some needs may be dormant, held in abeyance because more pressing needs are not being taken care of, or held in check because of the person's own expectations that such needs cannot be, or are unlikely to be, fulfilled.

What highly effective Leaders/Developers are able to do is to become aware of people's individual motivation patterns and needs, and connect with them. But they do more than that, at least the Transformational ones do. They bring out, and work with, the internal sources of motivation the individual has, not just the external ones of direct rewards; people start to motivate themselves and take increasing personal responsibility towards what become their own goals of developing higher performance. Instead of 'push', the approach then becomes a 'pull' one, with the Leader/Developer flexing their style appropriately. This is what development, and the Developing Stage is all about.



In Chapter 8, ways of reviewing and understanding individual motivation patterns will be more comprehensively explained.

| D3: | Generates Continuous Improvement | *Accepting responsibility for mistakes and realising that they will happen occasionally; dealing with them as learning opportunities; making consistent judgements about how much to become personally involved; concentrating on problem resolution rather than apportioning blame* |
|---|---|---|

This is about establishing, with the individual, continuous improvement as a way of life - so that it becomes a habit. Here, the way you deal with and accept responsibility for mistakes becomes crucial, for it is akin to being a hinge point in the process. If you react as though you didn't really believe they could do it, and grab back direction through command and control, people will realise very quickly that it is a game after all and you don't really trust them. If, however, you deal with the mistake as a learning opportunity, restoring confidence where necessary, then people will realise that you are for real and will be encouraged to progress further. It also builds the trust and support relationship.

Of course it is a very different situation if the mistake is due to carelessness, or lack of effort, or because the person doesn't want to or can't be bothered to do what is required. We are back to diagnosing performance issues. In such cases, where it is not a 'genuine' mistake, reprimands are appropriate. As part of situational consistency, too, it is sometimes appropriate to adjust your style to a more directive one if the person is not yet capable or willing to do what is required. But the way you handle the situation will be a real marker for the future.

It is also easy and tempting to pause at this stage. After all, you have achieved a lot. You have created movement and have made a difference, with people now on side and performing more effectively. But don't stop, keep continuous improvement going to its full fruition for the best is yet to come.



## 4. The Enabling Stage

> *"Start with the end in mind"*
>
> Covey

This is the fruition stage, the stage at which, when completed through the facilitation of the Leader/Developer, individuals and groups have not only the skills and knowledge to do what is required well, but the will and confidence to do so. They will be operating with Responsible Initiative, in fact, being appropriately self-directing, not only with the immediate tasks, but in a way where they take increasing ownership of their own continued learning to achieve personal mastery. It involves a new quality of partnership between the individuals concerned and the supporting Leader/Developer.

- ***Self-Direction and Responsible Initiative***

Self-directing people take Responsible Initiative in managing their own situations and in creating their own success. When they see a problem they take responsibility for ensuring it is dealt with, working out possible solutions and agreeing them, and promoting the right course of action, while taking other people's needs into account. They are effective '*high can do*' people.

This contrasts sharply with the Dependent or Counter Dependent behaviour (where initiative is often used irresponsibly) which you may well have experienced in the journey through the process to this stage. Dependent people always want to be told what to do and have problems solved for them (*'low can do'*), while Counter Dependent people are difficult to control and are dangerously unreliable, using initiative irresponsibly in a way in which they are unconcerned about or don't think through the consequences of what they do.



So the process is directed not just towards skills and knowledge, but also how these are applied in a self-sustaining, self-directing way. It parallels the stages of development of people as people, from childhood to a fully mature, capable and well-functioning person. The relevance is that because of the way people have often been managed at work, particularly where the style has been of a heavily 'command and control' or 'paternalistic' nature, or the culture has been power or role based, people can become habituated to Dependency or Counter Dependency.

| | |
|---|---|
| **Dependency** | Directed, nurtured and sustained by others |
| **Counter Dependency** | Rebelliousness; taking irresponsible initiative; being preoccupied with self |
| **Independency** | Taking care of self; becoming inner-directed and self-reliant; thinking own thoughts, making own decisions |
| **Interdependency** | Being self-reliant, proactive and capable, but also being able to join with and share the resources of other people |

Therefore, *'starting with the end in mind'* means developing the habits and attitudes of Responsible Initiative or, to put it another way, at least Independency and preferably Interdependency, rather than Dependency or Counter Dependency. We are back again to the underlying mindsets of *High Challenge-High Support* and *'I'm OK – You're OK' (I+U+)*.

Underlying Mindset and Resulting Behaviour:

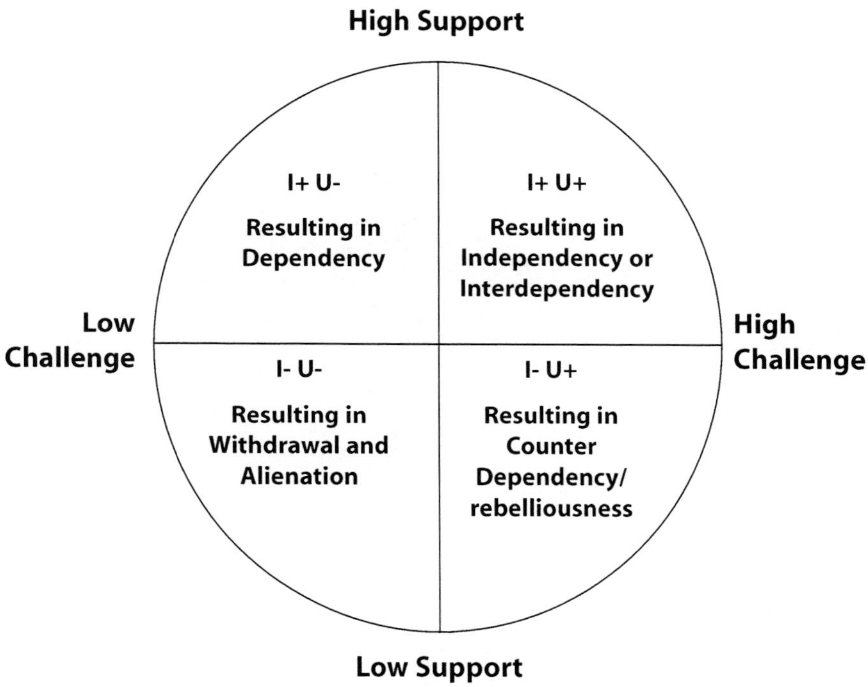




Why is this necessary and desirable? Firstly, you are very unlikely to create a high performing team without operating to this direction. It can be argued, of course, that in highly structured roles, or where the work is routine, being self-directing and using Responsible Initiative is not necessary. Such arguments are doubtful and, anyway, such roles are becoming increasingly rare. Secondly, because in the end it frees you (the Leader/Developer) up to apply your energies more fruitfully, rather than being overwhelmed by dealing with immediate problems. In today's fast moving world, people are increasingly required to move from the comfort zone and firm ground of the known, to cope with changing demands and requirements. This involves using their own judgement in applying new and lesser known areas of skill and knowledge, often in situations where there are no prescribed answers, and where they have to use Responsible Initiative in judging the right course of action. This is what makes for **competitive advantage through people.**

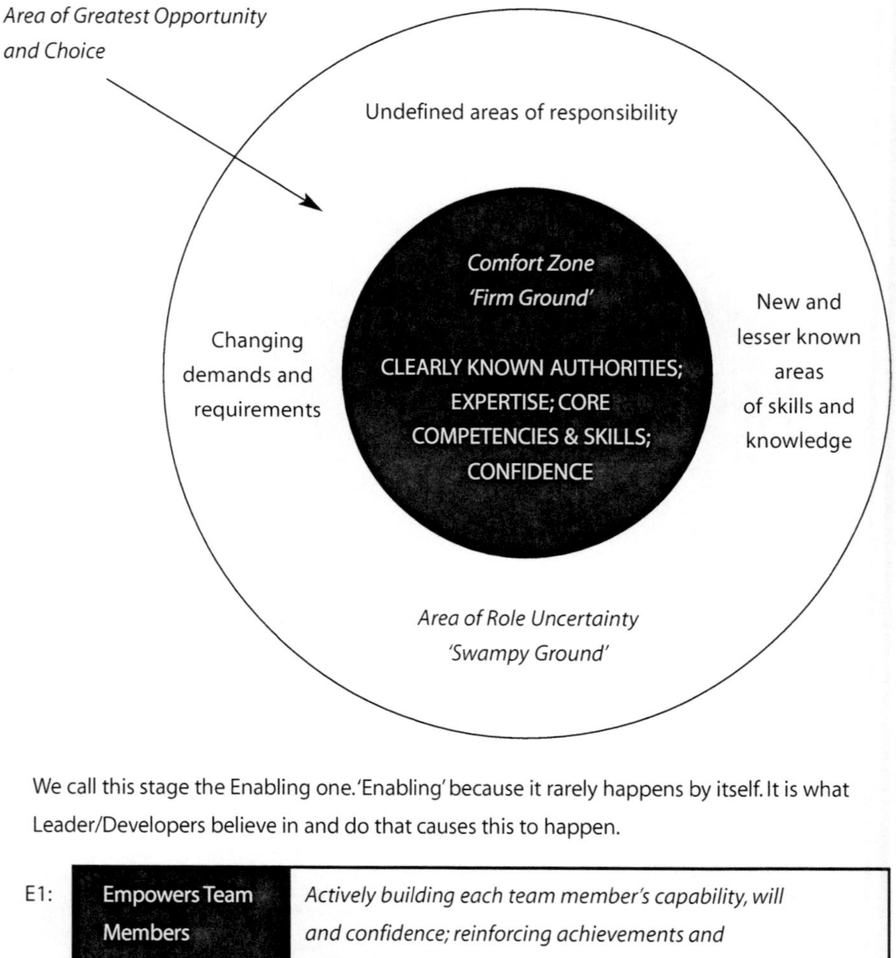




We call this stage the Enabling one. 'Enabling' because it rarely happens by itself. It is what Leader/Developers believe in and do that causes this to happen.

| E1: | Empowers Team Members | *Actively building each team member's capability, will and confidence; reinforcing achievements and enhancing performance and task ownership through coaching and mentoring* |
|---|---|---|

This is not leaving someone exposed to fail by leaving them to their own devices, but having prepared them with the necessary skills and knowledge, having reinforced their will to succeed, allowing people to try things out with increasing participation and involvement so their judgement and confidence is enhanced.

During all this, the style the Leader/Developer uses changes, becoming much less directive, and working with the person more on a 'partnership' basis than a 'tell' one.

This is the time when the person is about to fly solo, so to speak, and the Leader/Developer will need to have the generosity to 'let go', and demonstrate trust and confidence by getting their hands off the controls.

| E2: | Delegates Task Ownership | *Judging when individuals are ready to manage tasks by themselves, even though they may not recognise this; delegating authority while retaining responsibility if things go wrong; being prepared to let people make their own decisions to carry out the task their own way; keeping an eye on things at a discrete distance and only intervening when the situation goes badly wrong.* |
|---|---|---|



Delegation is the art of assigning authority and ownership for the completion of a task or specific activities to one of your team. For example, you might choose to delegate authority to make expenditures without direct approval from you – at least up to a stipulated amount. Or you may, say, give responsibility for checking their own work quality with someone who consistently demonstrates that their work is of the quality required. Delegation is a step, a major and fundamental one, in the direction of empowerment, which is wide and more embracing than delegating particular tasks. For, with empowerment, the person is given the power to use their own judgement in dealing with a whole series of issues; it requires the willingness to share power, and to do so effectively, on the part of both the Leader/Developer and team member. It requires the taking of Responsible Initiative.

The rationale for Delegation and Empowerment is quite straightforward and simple. With Delegation, at its most basic, the rationale is that no Leader can personally accomplish or completely supervise all the organisation's or department's tasks. To think otherwise is to fall into the trap of the old Command and Control school of thought. Appropriate Delegation frees the Leader up to concentrate on issues where their attention is best spent, as well as providing others with growth, development and rewards.

To get a better idea of what Delegation is, it is useful to look at what it is **not**. Delegation is not abdication in the sense of simply giving people jobs to do and telling them to get them done. If this kind of approach is taken you are unlikely to get the results that you want, because you are expecting people to guess what you want. Here **Explicitness** about the end results, the **What's**, matter greatly if you want the person to succeed; the **How's** of going about it is what is gifted to him or her. Likewise the Leader/Developer does not lose responsibility for the end results; s/he is accountable for what occurs, just as s/he is responsible for maintaining support throughout.



A surprising number of Leader/Developers experience difficulty, reluctance and discomfort in moving into Delegation. The barriers to Delegation which they express, offered here as a rationalisation, include:

**Barriers to Delegation**

- *I can do it better myself*
- *My people just aren't capable enough*
- *It takes too much time to explain what I want done*
- *If it goes wrong I'll still be accountable*
- *Delegation reduces my own authority*
- *I'll be shown up if they do too good a job*
- *My people prefer that I make the decisions*
- *Team members want to avoid responsibility (at work at least)*

*Ask yourself, which one of these, if any, applies to you?*

The **Real Reasons** for being unwilling to delegate are much more to do with:

- *I'm insufficiently organised or too inflexible to delegate efficiently*
- *I don't want to lose control*
- *I like people to be dependent on me*
- *I want to be the only expert*

| E3: | Provides Continuous Support | *Maintaining support, encouragement and reinforcement, sustaining and further developing team's High Performance* |
|---|---|---|



When a task or tasks are delegated, the Leader/Developer's job is not done – s/he still needs to be 'there' for the other person, providing continued support, encouragement, recognition and further development. One reason for this is that there will be other tasks that can increasingly be handed over, leading eventually to full empowerment and interdependence. The other is that it causes and provides **the relationship necessary for people to continue to both give of their best and develop and grow**.

This relationship requires building a level of trust between the two people: the Leader/Developer trusting the individual – who has demonstrated that s/he can be invested in – and the individual trusting the Leader/Developer and knowing s/he is on their side. Such trust needs to be invested wholeheartedly by the Leader/Developer but, if abused, the *High Challenge* side of the Leader/Developer will confront the situation, for trust involves mutuality and shared responsibility.

The process is one of '*support and verify*', not to catch the individual out, but to support their success, reinforcing it so that success through the full exercise of Responsible Initiative becomes the set of working habits.

The best Leader/Developers enable and empower others. On the other hand, Leaders who enjoy having dependent followers, like parents who exercise the power over their dependent children, cannot foster working relationships that will enable partnership and empowerment. They like to keep their people 'sapped' rather than 'zapping' them through the *High Challenge-High Support* approach.

## Sapping and Zapping

How you feel when you've been:

**Sapped**

- *Your job belongs to the company*
- *You are just doing whatever you are told*
- *Your job doesn't really matter*
- *You don't know how well you are doing*
- *You always have to keep your mouth shut*
- *Your job is something different from who you are*
- *You have little or no control over your work*

**Zapped**

- *Your job belongs to you*
- *You are responsible*
- *Your job counts for something*
- *You know where you stand*
- *You have some say in how things are done*
- *Your job is just part of who you are*
- *You have some control over your work*

From Zapp! The Lightning of Empowerment – WC Byham

So this is the Process of Developing High Performance and the skills involved, all of which is underpinned by the accompanying mindset of *High Challenge-High Support.* The skills are a mixture of those which are well known, and possibly well developed, and others which are less well known and not practiced so much. You will be able to conduct your own 'MOT Test', as it were, on your current skills, perhaps using the instruments provided, and through feedback from your own Leader and members of your team. In this way you can decide how to best focus your development energy. In the chapters that follow, skills will be dealt with in more detail.

What matters, too, is how the skills are used in combination. They are not exclusive to just one of the stages, they intertwine and reinforce each other throughout – Diagnosing Performance Issues is a skill, for example, that is of use during the Developing and Enabling Stages, as well as the Mobilising one. The process also gives a structured and consistent way of going about things so that direction and momentum is maintained, particularly as different individuals will go through it at different speeds. Some people may have reached the Enabling Stage while others are still at the Mobilising one, for example. Others may be at different stages for the differing tasks which make up their job.

Some of these skills and characteristics of the effective Leader/Developer are Transactional ones, others are Transformational ones.

The Transformational skills are those which feature in the Developing and Enabling Stages of the process, plus that part of Visioning which sees people performing at their very best and fulfilling their true performance potential. Although the term 'Transformational Leader' sounds as though heroic qualities are required, achieving such sustained High Performance and success is well within the grasp of the Leader/Developers who care enough to put themselves out to make it all happen. Of course, this involves developing and maintaining the attitudes and skills required within the process. It also means setting, for yourself, *High Challenge* and working to this.

It is the Transformational Leaders who achieve the Enabling stage with their people.
This is not to minimise the Transactional skills, much can be achieved with these alone. But, above all, Transformational Leaders start with 'the end in mind', seeing their people operating at their best and being the best they can be...

...what they 'vision' they cause to happen.

# Competencies for Leading & Developing High Performance

| VISIONING | | |
|---|---|---|
| V1 | **Consistency of Approach and Personal Style** | Projecting and holding a clear personal style and strong sense of who they are and what they stand for, which is clearly visible to others |
| V2 | **Observation and Information** | Listening and questioning effectively to establish facts and information; consulting with others to get views; perceptively observing differences between what is said and done, and where improvements can be made |
| V3 | **Analyses Present Situation Accurately** | Seeing above the waves; sifting information and forming views without jumping to conclusions; managing complexity without becoming submerged by it |
| V4 | **Creates a Future Vision** | Developing a clear, future sense of direction about what is to be done, which adds value; creating that vision for self and transmitting enthusiasm for and commitment to it; visioning everyone in the team performing at their best, being the best they can be |
| **MOBILISING** | | |
| M1 | **Provides Clarity and Explicitness** | Specifying in clear, unambiguous behavioural terms, what is required for successful operation, and what will be regarded as poor performance |
| M2 | **Maintains Own Assertiveness** | Applying appropriately the underlying skills and attitudes of assertiveness, necessary for being explicit and giving feedback, but also to maintain consistency of standards and approach; exerting strong leadership, when necessary, to prevent the team from going in different directions |
| M3 | **Gives Strong, Clear Feedback** | Giving feedback, both positive and negative, clearly and continuously, to reinforce positive results and correct the negative ones, in order to help the person to improve rapidly |

| MOBILISING | | |
|---|---|---|
| M4 | **Resiliently Retains Momentum and Direction** | Learns rapidly from events and experiences, is flexible in retaining overall vision, not thrown off course by setbacks and difficulties; keeps and resiliently pursues overall sense of direction |
| M5 | **Diagnoses Performance Issues Accurately** | Accurately diagnosing the root cause of an individual's performance issue, identifying the issue in specific behavioural terms and the underlying reasons, and deciding on a course of effective action to bring about the changes necessary |
| **DEVELOPING** | | |
| **D1** | **Flexes Style Appropriately: Is Situationally Consistent** | Deals with individuals on the basis of what they do not who they are; everyone knows clearly where they stand and that particular behaviours are responded to in consistent, particular ways; is able to flex style appropriately to deal with varying levels of performance and commitment to overall vision |
| D2 | **Knows Individuals Needs and Motivations** | Relating to team as individuals; realistic and knowledgeable about own and others' strengths and weaknesses; perceptive in knowing individuals' motivation patterns and needs and skilled in providing appropriate rewards |
| D3 | **Generates Continuous Improvement** | Accepting responsibility for mistakes and realising that they will happen occasionally; dealing with them as learning opportunities; making consistent judgements about how much to become personally involved, concentrating on problem resolution, rather than apportioning blame |

| ENABLING | | |
|---|---|---|
| E1 | **Empowers Team Members** | Actively building each team member's capability, will and confidence, reinforcing achievements and enhancing performance and task ownership through coaching and mentoring |
| E2 | **Delegates Task Ownership** | Judging when individuals are ready to manage tasks by themselves, even though sometimes they may not recognise this; delegating authority while retaining responsibility if things go wrong; being prepared to let people make their own decisions to carry out the task their own way; keeping an eye on things at a discrete distance and only intervening when the situation goes badly wrong |
| E3 | **Provides Continuous Support** | Maintaining support, encouragement and reinforcement, sustaining and further developing the team's High Performance. |

# Chapter Summary

- *Effective Leader/Developers follow a simple Four Step Process, underpinned and reinforced by the mind set and beliefs of High Challenge-High Support .*
- *The stages are the:* *Visioning Stage*
  *Mobilising Stage*
  *Developing Stage*
  *Enabling Stage*
- *They work to the principle of 'starting with the end in mind' and their 'vision' invariably includes, in their own words, seeing people operating at their very best and becoming the best they can be.*
- *More, they see their role in the Process as enabling people to lose their Dependency, and instead becoming Interdependent and operating with Responsible Initiative.*
- *be Leaders/Developers, recognising that they are part of the situation and define that situation. This means they cause things to happen.*
- *Further, as well as having the necessary Transactional skills, they have and use Transformational ones. They motivate people to achieve and develop much more than was originally thought possible, by connecting people to the energy of their own internal motivation and needs, so that they become Self-Directing.*
- *They work on the <u>both/and</u> basis of Vision and Action. Vision without Action is just a dream, and Action without Vision is meaningless and boring.*
- *Successful completion of the Process is a step by step, little and often, cumulative process, with people proceeding through it at different rates, and the Leader/Developer flexing his/her style according to where people are in the process.*
- *There are a number of skills and competencies involved at each stage. Some of these skills are well known and are likely to be well developed, others are less well known and are likely to need to be developed. The skills set is best applied as an integrated, combined whole.*

- *The skills and competencies required are:*

1. ***Visioning Stage***

   *V1: Visibility of Personal Style*

   *V2: Observation and Information*

   *V3: Analysis*

   *V4: Vision*

2. ***Mobilising Stage***

   *M1: Clarity and Explicitness*

   *M2: Assertion*

   *M3: Feedback*

   *M4: Momentum*

   *M5: Diagnosing Performance Issues*

3. ***Developing Stage***

   *D1: Situational Consistency*

   *D2: Motivation*

   *D3: Continuous Improvement*

4. ***Enabling Stage***

   *E1: Empowers*

   *E2: Delegation*

   *E3: Continued Support*

- *The most effective Leader/Developers have strong Developing and Enabling skills as well as Visioning and Mobilising ones.*

chapter 4

# Explicitness: The Under-Emphasised Skill

- *What Explicitness Is and Why It Is Helpful*
- *Why People Are Sometimes Reluctant To Be Explicit*
- *The 'Onion Model'*
  - *as a way of seeing the important differences between Personality, Values, Attitudes and Behaviours*
- *The Skills of Explicitness and When To Use Them*

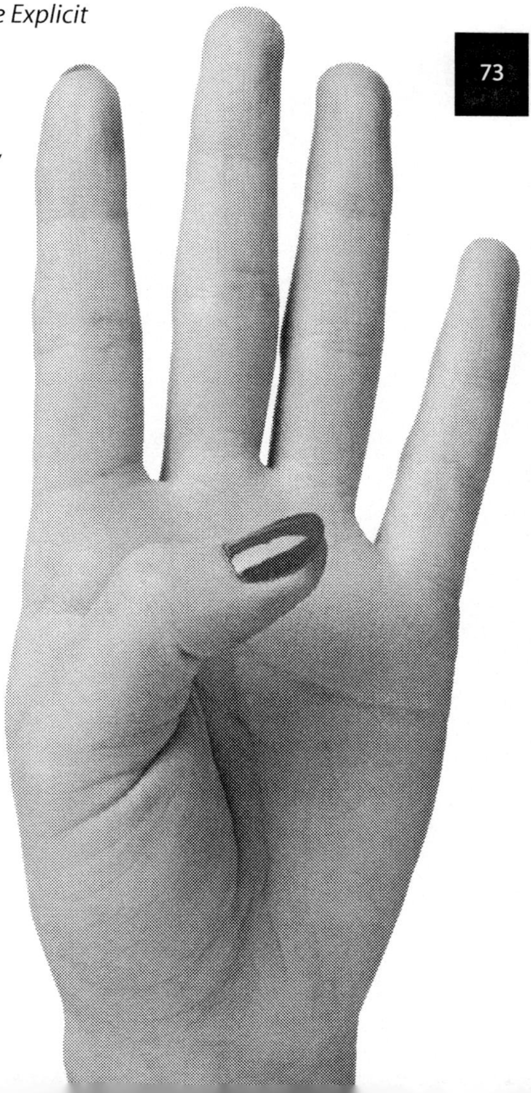

# What Explicitness Is and Why It is Helpful

| M1: | Provides Clarity and Explicitness | *Specifying in clear, unambiguous, behavioural terms, what is required for successful operation, and what will be regarded as poor performance* |
|---|---|---|

Imagine that you are responsible for teaching a small child to cross the road. Would you take that child to the M25 and say to the child something like, *"The objective of the exercise is to cross the road and then return safely, now off you go and let me know how you get on."* Of course you wouldn't, the consequences don't bear thinking about! Yet this is analogous to the approach which many managers adopt when briefing their staff about what they require them to do.



The highly effective Leader/Developers we worked with, however, used well a fundamental skill which was a basis for their success. Yet this skill is rarely taught, rarely mentioned in management texts, and it is assumed that most people who lead groups have it. They don't or don't use it. This is the skill of defining and communicating in **unambiguous behavioural** terms exactly what performance they want. They fail to achieve the performance they require because they haven't thought through, explicitly, what they require and/or don't communicate this explicitly. Sometimes this is done under the mistaken belief that to do so is patronising. It isn't – on the contrary, it can be particularly helpful, especially during the Mobilising Stage.

The first thing to understand about Explicitness is that it focuses on behaviour, rather than the personality or values of the person. A very useful way of crystallising this is through the 'Onion' model.

# The Onion Model

## Personality, Values, Attitudes and Behaviours

If it is necessary for an individual to increase their performance or to develop their skills in a particular area, a change is required. For some people this change appears to be unachievable as, at first sight, it seems to require them to be something they are not, and as a result the change does not happen.

This same view can often be a barrier to the Leader/Developer who may hesitate from delivering the total message for fear of damaging sensibilities, or of expecting a total shift in someone's personality.

> *"I need Mark to show more initiative, but I can't tell him as he's not that sort of person"*



The Onion model illustrates how people are made up of different layers, and how, by focusing on the required changes to **behaviour**, it makes the message much more effective and easier to give. It is also easier for the recipient to take in and act on.

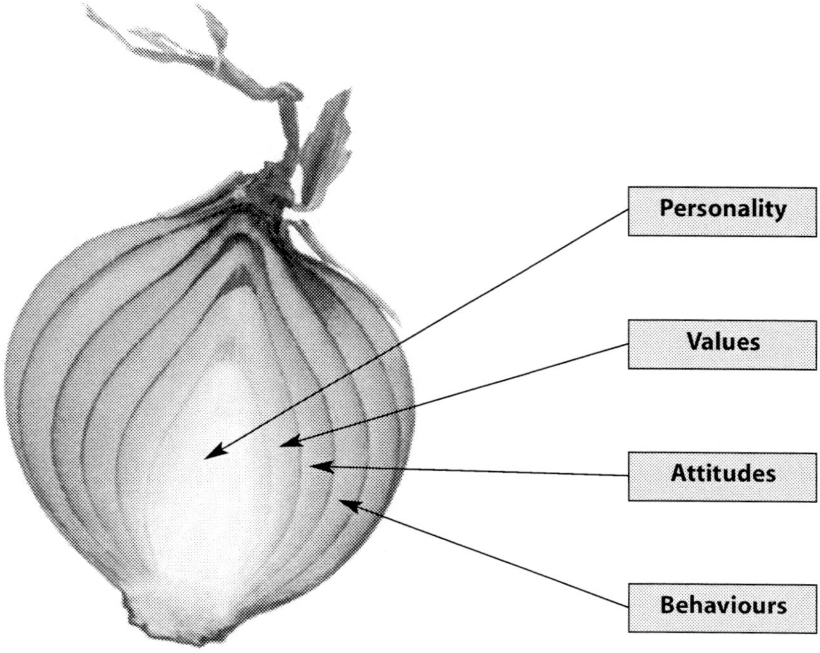

- ***Personality***

  *At the core of a person is their Personality. This is largely set in adults, and it is not within the Leader/Developer's rights or abilities to try to change someone's Personality. Personality is someone's inner being, the integral self. To criticise this inner being is experienced as attacking the person and will provoke a negative and unproductive response.*

- ***Values***

  *These are a person's deep-seated beliefs which are relatively enduring and connected with their personality. They are the way the person makes sense of the world and provide an essential modus operandi for the way they lead their life. They, too, form an integral part of the person's being.*



  *Values are not readily changed in the normal course of events. Where there is disagreement between two people, it will not be resolved by one trying to change the other's Values. Again this will be experienced as attacking the person's integral self and will result in defensiveness and resistance.*

  *An underlying approach to take when dealing with others is that of having Positive Regard for them as individuals. This means accepting, respecting and valuing the integral self of the other person. It means holding and projecting the view that the other person is OK and having a positive belief in them as a person. If this is not the case, then the person will feel 'written off' or 'disliked', instead of being valued.*

> *The outer layers of the Onion Model are Attitudes and Behaviours. These are more to do with what an individual actually says and does, rather than who they are. It is at this level that problems can be addressed and changes more readily effected.*

- ***Attitudes***

  *Attitudes are the underlying beliefs or approaches to work and life which underpin behaviour. They are less deep-rooted than Values, and can change. For example, a team member might have an attitude about a particular type of work, stemming from their own belief, that it is of little importance or not valued. Their Attitude can change completely, in this instance, if someone demonstrates why this work is important and how it benefits the organisation.*

- ***Behaviours***

  *This is what people actually do. How they handle clients, brief their teams, appraise their staff, etc. Behaviours are visible to all, and the acquisition of the right behaviours appropriate to the situation, underpinned by supporting attitudes, is what leads to improved performance.*

*It is important then to concentrate on the Behaviours and Attitudes displayed by the team member – what they do – NOT who they are.*



*The attitude of Positive Regard, which is key, helps reinforce that...*

***...underneath the Behaviours leading to poor performance there is a person to be valued and who deserves Explicitness to allow them to make the changes required.***

# The Skills of Explicitness and When To Use Them

Explicitness then is defining, and specifying in explicit behavioural terms, what is required, so that the person has a clear mental picture of the actions, behaviour or results that …

- *are required for effective performance*
- *lead to poor performance and are unhelpful*

…. and where these definitions of expected behaviour are specific and not general or ambiguous.

Phrases such as "*You need to adopt a more positive attitude*" or "*You need to work on your client relations*" are not very helpful. They leave the recipient with a plethora of possible meanings and actions to take, only one of which is going to address the problem as it is actually seen by the Leader/Developer.

The key to Explicitness is the ability to define, in unambiguous behavioural terms, exactly what performance is positive and to be encouraged, and what is a problem and needs to be changed. In this latter case, not only does what is said is needed to address the problem behaviours, but also to explicitly detail the behaviours that are desirable and would counteract the problem.

To illustrate the point, the following two scenarios show two possible approaches to dealing with the same situation:

- ***Scenario 1:***

> *"One problem area we need to look at is your communication with your colleagues. You really need to keep them in the picture more so there are no nasty surprises lurking. The X project is a case in point – I'm sure you know what I mean."*

- ***Scenario 2:***

> *"One area I need to tell you about that is causing me problems is your communication with me and others working with you on projects. I'd like to use the X project as an example of what I mean."*
>
> *"Your initial briefing to us was fine – it had clear terms of reference and deadlines and our individual responsibilities were clearly delineated. I found that particularly helpful."*
>
> *"However, when the deadline was brought forward, you didn't tell me. This caused problems with resources and meant that I had to drop two options that might have been useful to the client. I know that deadlines shift, but what would help next time would be if you called a short meeting as soon as you hear of a change, and ensure that we all hear the same message and can re-schedule the work together."*
>
> *"There is one other point I would like to mention that came out of the X project – at the meeting when we discussed contingencies, you seemed not to be listening. You were continually looking at your watch and left the meeting twice to answer your mobile. Contingency plans were agreed but none of us felt that you fully understood the implications or the costs. You gave no sign that you were satisfied with the outcome and, as a result, we were uncertain how to proceed. I feel that it would have been helpful for you to summarise what was said and produce a short note detailing the changes so that we could be confident about proceeding."*



Scenario 2, in this case, is far more likely to achieve results as specific behavioural issues were addressed. The recipient is clear about what s/he had done to cause the problem and what s/he needs to do in the future. Although Scenario 2 here is longer, it is surprising how often being explicit takes less time, particularly in the long run.

Explicitness gives clarity. It also gives choice because the issues are made clear. Its very clarity and directness gives it a power which, by itself, is likely to produce results. It may be this very power which inhibits people from being explicit, coupled with a possible confusion that Personality and Values are part of the arena. They are not, the arena is Behaviour only, and being specific about what is required is legitimate, helpful and inoffensive when delivered properly. The way it is delivered has to be from the I+U+ position of two adults dealing with a situation. Even when the Behaviour is one which needs to be corrected, it is not the person who is at fault – they are still OK – the issue is their Behaviour, on this occasion. You still have Positive Regard for them, demonstrably so in that you are Genuine in being clear about what you mean and meaning what you say.



Explicitness is particularly useful in the initial stage of the process where there needs to be emphasis on **'what'** needs to be done and **'how'** to do it. In the latter stages of the process, the emphasis will change; clarity on the **'What's'** is still required but a lot more discretion and participation is encouraged with the **'How's'**.

Explicitness too is the starting point for diagnosing performance issues, which we will explore in Chapter 5.

# Chapter Summary

- *Explicitness is a key skill, core to Leading and Developing High Performance.*
- *Explicitness is the skill of defining in* ***unambiguous behavioural*** *terms exactly what is required in terms of performance.*
- *Carried out correctly, Explicitness is helpful - not insulting or patronising – as it positions the person to succeed.*
- *Explicitness focuses on Behaviour, not someone's Personality or Values as described in the 'Onion' model. Personality and Values are not amenable to change, and will be experienced anyway as a personal attack. Addressing Behaviours, what someone actually does, is legitimate, focuses on what matters and is less threatening, and makes it easier to be acted upon.*
- *Explicitness then is concerned with defining behaviourally what is...*
  - required for effective performance
  - undesirable and will be disapproved of...

  *...in specific, not general or ambiguous, terms, so the person has a clear mental picture of what is required.*

# chapter 5

# Diagnosing Performance Issues

## Why People Behave As They Do

- *Sources of Behaviour*
- *Diagnosing the Root Cause of Performance Issues*
- *Diagnostic Flow Chart: 15 Steps*
- *Description of the 15 Steps with Examples*
- *Case Study*
- *Chapter Summary*



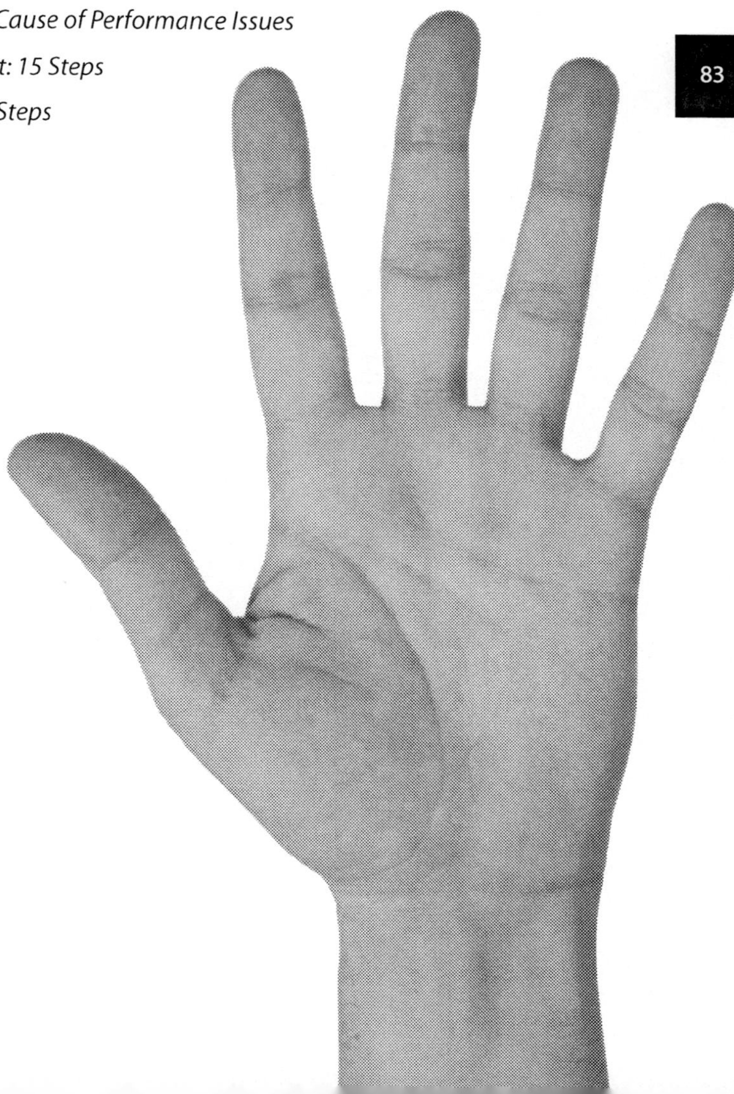

# Sources of Behaviour

Most of us have learned to become adept at diagnosing performance issues in our area of technical or specialist expertise. If a piece of equipment is not working properly, or a system is failing, or there are persistent quality problems, what we do is to diagnose the root cause of such problems. We know that to solve the problem we have to diagnose that problem accurately – there is no point in proceeding otherwise, and we have help available in diagnosing these types of problems using a range of techniques – eg, brainstorming, 'herringbone' diagrams, etc.

When it comes to diagnosing 'people' problems, however, we are often much less adept, and tend to resort to a level of generalisation such as saying "It's an *attitude* problem" or a "*training/development*" issue. This is not terribly accurate or helpful in moving things forward. What is necessary is a way of identifying what the problem really is and the reasons for it occurring.



The difficulty may be that people are seen as much more complicated and unpredictable than 'things' (they are, thank goodness), but there are still ways of understanding what is going on and why. This can be done without getting immersed too deeply in the mystical realms of psychology, rather to remain in the Behaviour and Attitudes arena.

People aren't daft – they do things for a reason. Identifying the reason is the most important part of the diagnosis process. In starting to explore the source of these reasons, there is an old Hungarian Fable which has much to teach us.

*A man was out fishing, in a boat, on a lake. It was a beautiful day and the fisherman was feeling pleased with the world. There was a tug on his line, and when he reeled it in there was a snake – and the snake had a live frog in its mouth.*

*Feeling sorry for the frog, the fisherman took it from the snake and threw the frog back in the water Then he felt that perhaps that had not been fair on the snake, so he looked around the boat to see what he could give the snake. All he had was a bottle of brandy, so he gave the snake a slug of brandy then threw the snake back in the water.*

*Ten seconds later, there was a loud knocking on the side of the boat, and there was the snake again – this time with two frogs in its mouth.*

The point of this story is that...

- *What gets rewarded gets done*
- *You get more of the behaviours you reward... and*
- *It is easy to inadvertently reward the wrong thing*

# Diagnosing the Root Cause of Performance Issues

People tend to do things they find rewarding, and avoid doing things where there is a negative consequence or payoff for them. The reasons we do or don't do something is much influenced by the perceived rewards, or penalties, which flow from our actions. Yet as Leaders we are often guilty of rewarding inappropriate behaviour, such as not giving the worst jobs to those who complain most, but instead to those who complain least; giving the most attention to people who perform poorly and not those who perform highly, or 'punishing' someone for under-spending their budget by inappropriately reducing their budget the following year.

Other key factors in diagnosing performance issues are whether the person knows clearly what is expected *(Explicitness)*, and whether they are doing what they are doing because they don't have the skills and knowledge required *(Can't Do)*, or whether they do have the capability but choose not to exercise it *(Won't Do)*. These are the basic tools for Diagnosing Performance Issues.

It helps, though, to have a disciplined process to follow – a flow chart in fact. Sometimes there is a measure of stress in the situation, and when this is the case it becomes even more important to have a clear, rational way to diagnose what is going on. It is rather like dealing with a failed diesel engine in a boat at sea – the law seems to be that engines break down when you need them most. It is so easy to get confused, or jump to the wrong conclusion, to start stripping the engine down perhaps, when a glance at the diagnostic flow chart in the owner's manual gives a logical sequence to work to – 'check to see if there is fuel in the tank' is better done before stripping the engine down than afterwards. Of course, experienced mechanics become so familiar with the process that they don't have to use the manual – so you will become in diagnosing people performance issues if you follow the process to be suggested.

Initially, though, it is useful to build up your diagnostic skills by adopting the discipline of working through the flow chart stage-by-stage. Eventually, it will become part of you, and because your subsequent action will be based on an accurate diagnosis, you will become highly effective in resolving performance issues.

The approach is not just confined to remedying poor performance, it is equally valuable in developing further already good performance, or helping someone through transition and change. One very important point is the need to take early, rather than late, action when you see a performance issue developing. The risk with not intervening early is that new habits can form, or the inappropriate behaviour becomes entrenched, making it much more difficult to deal with and resolve later on.

We will be dealing with the Rewards and Negative Consequences (or Penalties) available to the Leader/Developer of High Performance in Chapter 6. What is important, at this stage, is to stress that we are not talking about pots of gold, or whips (usually unavailable to the modern leader anyway), but instead a rich source of subtle and lighter approaches, as the following example will illustrate.

*Jane, who was at one time Practice Manager in a small Consultancy Practice, had no direct authority over Tim, one of the Partners. At the end of each month, Jane had to deal with the expenses submitted by each Partner. The problem she had was that Tim regularly sent in his expenses several weeks late. Jane decided to do something about this.*

*She talked to Tim and told him that his lateness was causing her a problem. Tim's attention was immediately caught because he got on well with Jane. Then she told him that his lateness was interrupting the time she was able to spend with her children. Again, this had a strong affect because Tim had children the same age as Jane's, and he was a strong family man. However, she knew that Tim, despite his good intentions, would still leave his expenses on the kitchen table when the sun shone, or there were more interesting things for him to do. So, she told him that Dick (another Partner who Tim worked with a lot) always got his expenses in on time. That provided the real incentive.*

*The next month end, Tim phoned Jane to see whether he had beaten Dick (who knew nothing about all this at the time). "Not quite, but you're within distance" was the reply. The next month when Tim phoned it was. "Nearly, it was close, but Dick just beat you". The following month Tim 'cracked' it. He got from Jane a simple card with a big gold star on it, like children are given at school, with the message "Well Done Tim, you've beaten Dick!"'.*

*Tim's expenses have never since been sent to Jane significantly late.*

This story also illustrates one other factor concerning performance. Inconvenience to other person, even when that other person is liked and respected, is usually not a sufficient spur to act to remove such inconvenience for the other person. The intentions may be good, but often the action does not consistently follow through. It is only when the inconvenience is experienced by the person not performing as required, such as through the lack of reward or the experiencing of penalties, that action starts to happen.

At this stage, though, we will concentrate on diagnosing the cause of the particular performance issue, using the flow chart shown on page 89 as the diagnostic tool, and exploring each step in the process.

# Diagnostic Flow Chart

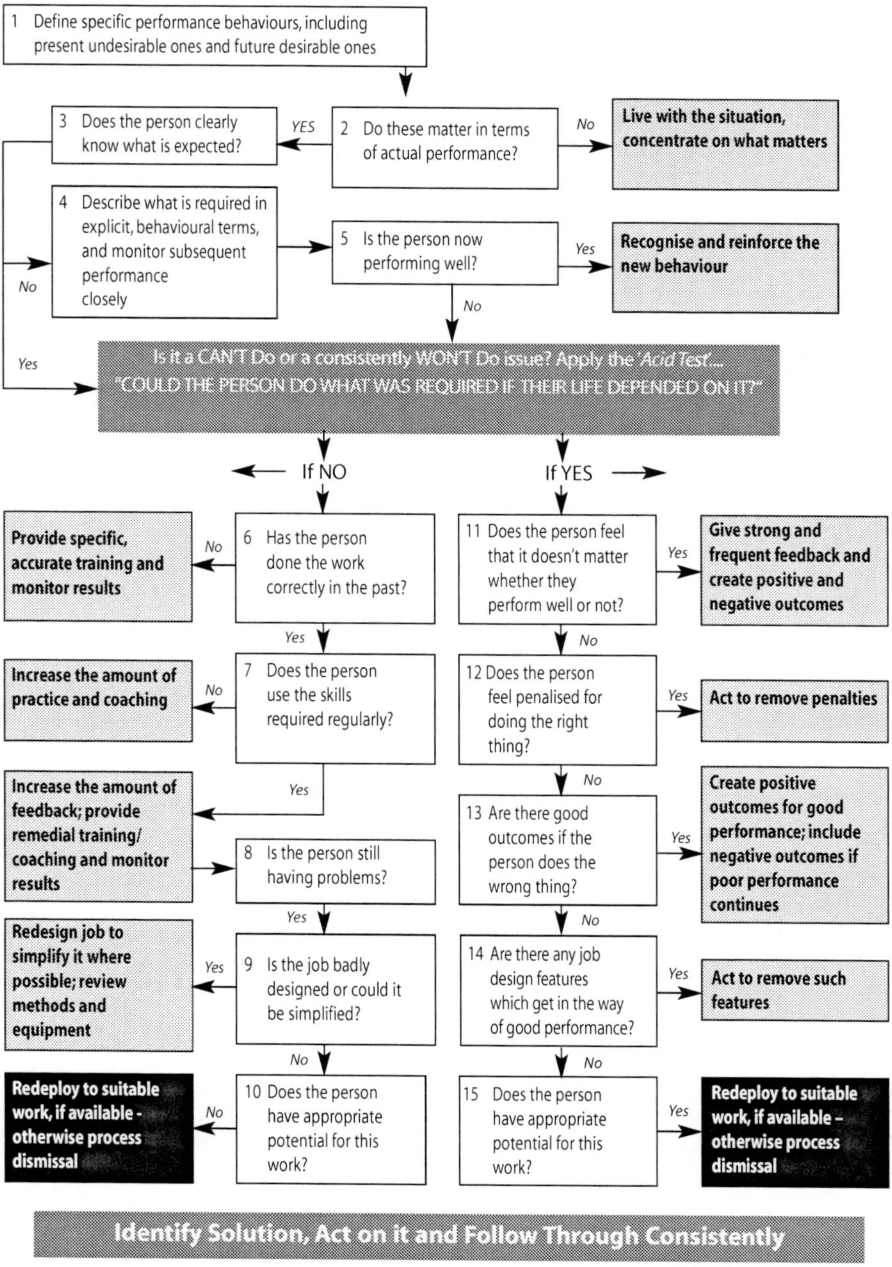


89

# Description of the 15 Steps with Examples

## 1. Define the specific performance behaviours, including present undesirable ones and future desirable ones

This is the essential starting position. The accuracy of the diagnosis will depend on this stage, just as a physician starts with the symptoms of an illness instead of dangerously leaping to conclusions about the nature of the illness.

For symptoms we can read *Behaviours* – what the person is or is not doing – defined in clear, explicit, behavioural terms. It is the outer ring, the Behaviour one of the Onion Model, that matters at this stage; it enables what is actually happening (observable facts) to be captured and identified. It is the way to unravel those sometimes seemingly intractable or complex problems and to get a handle on them so you can proceed with clarity and confidence.



We are not talking here just of poor performers. Many existing good performers could turn in an even better performance by improving in one or two areas; other people are still developing and growing and will do so more surely and quickly with this approach.
In addition, the process is very useful in helping people manage change and transition, for moving through it one step at a time and successfully completing the process so that they end up more competent and capable than they were at the beginning.

Some performance issues may seem overwhelmingly large, swamping you with their very scale and seeming complexity. The way to proceed is one step at a time so that cumulatively, over time, and through reinforcement, major changes can be achieved. In these cases it is often best to concentrate, initially, on those immediate behavioural changes which will have greatest effect.

At first, until the process becomes an integral part of the way you work, it pays to write down the present undesirable behaviours *(less of)* and the future desirable ones *(more of)*. Going through this discipline will also concentrate your mind on getting to the essence of the issue, at the same time preparing you for the discussion with the individual once you have completed the diagnosis and decided your course of action.

## 2. Do these matter in terms of actual performance?

This is where you have to be honest with yourself. It may be that the scale of the 'problem' does not matter in terms of actual performance, that somehow it has got out of proportion. Take the person, for example, who produces £10K of good quality business every month, but is always a day late in submitting it. Or where the issue irritates the hell out of you personally – perhaps a speech habit or mannerism – but which really does not matter in terms of actual performance. Then again, you may occasionally find fault with the other person because, basically, they are not like you, forgetting, for the moment, that it is what they actually do – their performance and behaviour – which is the issue.

The other side of the coin is to pretend that something does not matter, when it does (to 'cop out' in fact), or to maintain that all your people are 'perfect' and are working to their full potential. This does no-one any favours, not the organisation, not the individuals concerned, not yourself. Or it may be that one of your people is doing a good, reliable job, but wants to stay in the security of their comfort zone and not take on anything new. Is this acceptable into the future, or will it inhibit their future security or the team's performance?



The question to be answered is whether the behaviour matters in terms of High Performance. If the answer is NO, then the action is for you to live with the situation, concentrating on what does matter; if the answer is YES (which most often is the case), then the question in step 3 must be addressed.

## 3. Does the person clearly know what is expected?

Quite simply, if the person doesn't clearly know what is expected, then whether they succeed or not is a matter of chance, of accident. The need for the Mobilising skills of Explicitness were described earlier; without Explicitness, in the early stages, people are not positioned to succeed – rather they are positioned to fail. If the person does not clearly know what is expected and is not performing well because of this, then the fault and responsibility is primarily yours.

This applies even when people have work delegated to them or are working in an 'empowered' way. There is an important distinction here between knowing the standards and outputs required, and the judgements and actions an individual takes to achieve these. Both delegation and empowerment require Explicitness about standards and outputs required, even if it is mostly concerned with working to certain operating principles and values. Without this, people will be working in the dark. Mistakes, genuine ones, will happen when judgements are made and this is a part of learning. It is only when such mistakes are persistent that more remedial approaches, involving perhaps a different leadership style, come into play (see Chapter 9).

*Have you ever explicitly detailed what is needed (not just left it to common sense)?*

Ask yourself whether the person involved clearly knows what is expected. If the answer is YES, perhaps because you have briefed that person explicitly several times in the recent past, then you need to move on to the next stage in the flow chart. If the answer is NO, then you will need to concentrate on stage 4.



### 4. Describe what is required in explicit, behavioural terms, and monitor subsequent performance closely

In many situations the simple and straightforward act of describing what is required in explicit, behavioural terms, of addressing the issue firmly and assertively but with Positive Regard, and to do so early on before the situation becomes embedded, will be sufficient.

When people know what is and what is not required, and there is no discretion about it, providing they have the capability they will often quite simply deliver to these requirements, "If that's what you want, that's what you'll get". Of course, this only applies when the issue is addressed at the Behaviour level, and not at the Values or Personality ones.

Where people are moving through the transition of change, such Explicitness is also helpful and enabling, for the Explicitness provides clarity and certainty, where before there may have existed only confusion and ambiguity. With development and coaching, too, it is often appropriate – the focus here being more on outputs and standards rather than how to achieve them, while with poor or inexperienced performers, there will need to be emphasis on both outputs/standards and the behavioural 'How's' of achieving them.

The preparation done in stage 1 will prove to be very valuable here. Remember that what is required will have been described in explicit behavioural terms, when the person clearly understands the actions, behaviour and results that are...

- *required and expected*
- *not desired and are inappropriate, and*
- *where these are specific, not general or ambiguous*

It is not enough to leave things at this stage; there is a need to follow through and monitor subsequent performance closely, not just the once, but sufficiently to ensure that the person not only understands and is capable of doing what is required, but has absorbed the new learning or habits consistently into their work pattern. This leads to step 5 in the flow chart.

## 5. Is the person now performing well?

If the answer is YES, then this needs to be recognised and reinforced through appropriate feedback (as will be discussed in Chapter 7). It may also be the time to take the next step of another incremental change or piece of development, building on the person's success thus far.



If the person is NOT now performing well – or the answer to stage 3 was YES – the issue lies at a deeper level of analysis.

*When people know what is required and their performance consistently does not reach this level, one of two sets of reasons will apply (with just occasionally a mix of the two):*

***They CAN'T Do*** ...that is, they don't have the skills/ knowledge/competence required

***They WON'T Do*** ...that is, they don't have the Will to do what is required, or choose not to – sometimes called Attitude

*There is an 'Acid Test' which is highly useful in analysing whether the issue is a Can't Do or a Won't Do one...*

***Could the person do what is required if their life depended on it?***

- *If the answer is NO then it is a Skills issue*
- *If the answer is YES then it is an Attitude/Will issue*

The majority of poor performance issues, in our experience at least, are Won't Do ones; that is, the people concerned would meet the standards required if their lives depended on it – **provided they knew clearly what was expected**. They could do it if they had to!

The tendency, however, is to answer the issue as a Can't Do one, maybe because it's often an easier option, maybe through being over-generous in giving the benefit of the doubt, maybe because it is too much trouble to assume anything else. Leader/ Developers who have a strong inclination to Support are prone to do this, whereas those with a strong Challenge bias are more likely to assume that issues are generally Won't Do ones. This is where using the idea of the High Challenge-High Support approach is so important – to ensure that the issue is faced for what it is. Operating to this diagnostic framework, too, will give the rigour to analyse, accurately, the source of the problem and then go on to resolve it.



If the issues are in the Won't Do arena, there will be a payoff for the people concerned, either in the form of some rewards or the avoidance of perceived negative outcomes, so it is important to find out the reasons for their behaviour. As was described in the Frog Fable, what gets rewarded gets done, and it is easy to inadvertently reward the wrong thing, as we will see.

Firstly, though, we will follow the Can't Do route through the flow chart.

# *CAN'T DO (SKILLS) ISSUES*

### 6. Has the person done the work correctly in the past?

If the answer is NO, then basically the responsibility for the poor performance is yours, and the way the person is dealt with will be different to that used in a Won't Do situation, as will be described in more detail in Chapter 7.

The action is to provide specific, accurate training and to monitor the results. Training here does not necessarily mean courses; there will be a range of options available to you, including personal tuition, coaching, 'on-the-job' instruction or arranging for someone who does the work well to enskill the person. The approach, too, will need to reflect the person's general level of competence and experience. Whether you carry out the training yourself or not, you will need to monitor the results, to make sure that the person is now meeting the performance required.



*In one case we came across, a new appointee who was very knowledgeable about the product, did not seem to be able to sell it, although he got on famously with prospective clients who welcomed his opinion. In order to make a sale he had to access computer records to check prices and stock availability, but did not know how to do so and was ashamed to admit it (he had previously been a Director in a smaller firm which had been absorbed into the Group). When his Leader had analysed the problem and realised what was going on, and given him three hours hands-on training, the 'poor performer', within a year, became one of the top performing salesmen in the Region.*

If the answer is YES, that is, the person has carried out the work correctly in the recent past and the level of performance is not sufficient, then we need to explore step 7.

### 7. Does the person regularly use the skills required?

Sometimes people get rusty if the skill required is not used regularly. In this case, it is not as though the person can't do it, it's more a case of getting back to speed and quality, and perhaps confidence. Here extensive re-training involving starting from scratch is probably not required; what will be necessary, though, will be to increase the amount of practice and coaching, with plenty of reassurance. Don't let the person stumble on.

> *For example, you may have passed your driving test with flying colours – several years ago. Could you pass that same test in an hour from now? This isn't to suggest that you can't drive well, but passing the driving test probably requires brushing up on those procedures, and skills and knowledge, particular to the test. What is the stopping distance in the wet when driving at 60mph, for instance?*



If the person does the task regularly, and has done the work correctly in the recent past, and their performance has deteriorated, the first thing to check out is whether it is still a Skills issue and whether the skills need recalibrating. What can happen is that bad skill habits can develop, or the person may not realise that their standards have slipped. Here the action is firstly to increase the amount of feedback, as a result of which the performance problem may become self-correcting. If this does not happen you will need to provide remedial training or coaching, and then, importantly, to monitor the results.

This brings us to step 8.

### 8. Is the person still having problems?

If the person is still having problems, there is one further step to check out, providing that you are still sure that the problem is in the Can't Do rather than the Won't Do category. Hang on to your perseverance - some people are hares and others tortoises, the tortoise can complete the same journey in the end and can then turn in a solidly consistent good performance. Equally, if you are developing someone to take on a new set of skills, you may have caused that person to struggle with a chunk of learning that is just too large for them to grasp.

## 9. Is the job badly designed, or could it be simplified?

Sometimes a job is so poorly designed that the design itself affects good performance.

> *In one case, a production line team found that after a work method readjustment, they were physically unable to carry out the required tasks, despite being skilled and experienced operators who had previously performed well.*

Often the job can be simplified, or aids thought of as a way of helping someone to perform it well, such as the piece of learning 'chunked down' into a more digestible bite – enabling progress. It is important to check the job design before moving on to the next stage.



## 10. Does the person have appropriate potential for this work?

The person has tried – it's not a case of Won't Do but Can't Do. You have done all you can to enable the person to succeed, have followed the steps, given time and attention, acted with High Challenge-High Support.

What is crucial is to maintain the perspective of High Challenge-High Support. You will be sorry for the individual but you will be doing him/her, yourself, your team and the organisation no favours by carrying on. It will be debilitating for the individual and overall performance.

People have different kinds of potential - not everyone can be a brain surgeon (not least because a number of us faint at the sight of blood!). Perhaps a more common example is that of selling, where, despite trying so hard to succeed that it causes stress, some people find selling is not for them. The person is still OK and needs to be treated with Positive Regard. The particular kind of work is not suitable for them, that is all; other kinds will suit them better. Redeploy the person to more suitable work, if possible, if not you will need to move towards severance, while doing all you can to maintain that person's dignity and self respect. They (and you) have tried, it's not a Won't Do but a **Can't Do**.

It may sound harsh, but not dealing with the situation is likely to prove harsher still in the long run.

## WON'T DO (ATTITUDE) ISSUES

We'll return now to the Won't Do part on the flow chart, where the person is capable of doing what is required, but somehow doesn't do so consistently or can't be relied upon to do so. In these situations, people are operating to an agenda of their own as there will be a pay-off for them of some kind – it may be some form of reward or may be to avoid negative outcomes or penalties. These can be subtle, as we will see, such as preferring to stay within the security of a comfort zone rather than experiencing the discomfort of moving outside it.



**11. Does the person feel that it doesn't matter whether they perform well or not?**

If the person feels that it doesn't matter, then this is the classic situation of *Low Challenge-Low Support*, resulting in apathy and low commitment. From the Leader/Developer's point of view it's also a classic example of 'you get what you give'.

People who are left in this position, despite perhaps their early good intentions, will find it increasingly difficult to maintain a good performance in such a void. This is particularly so when the norms of the group to which they belong are that 'it doesn't matter'. In this situation, without feedback and stimulation, what people do at work loses meaning and satisfaction, and they will find it increasingly difficult to invest of themselves in it. Here there are no rewards, or recognition, if people do a good job, neither are there penalties or comeback (another form of recognition) if they perform poorly – so why bother?

As we will see, recognition of what we do is so important for the great majority of people; without recognition it is as though we don't exist. Classic 'jobs-worth' behaviour – *"It's more than my job's worth"* – the antithesis of empowerment, often results from the attitudes thus developed.

Here the message is keep your nose clean, keep a low profile, don't inconvenience yourself, don't do anything that can go wrong, do just what the rules say – you won't be thanked for doing anything different and you won't get into trouble.

The crucial point is that it has to matter to the individual concerned, and this can be achieved through appropriate rewards and penalties. Take an individual, for example, who has to draft a report each month on behalf of the Leader. The report is often of such poor quality, or late, that the Leader ends up writing it, staying behind to do so and not addressing the performance issue with the staff member. It doesn't matter to the individual here whether s/he performs or not, the report may seem to him/her to be of little consequence. It is only when there are consequences to **the individual** that timelines and quality will be improved.

A common cause of Leaders operating in a way which cause people to feel that it doesn't matter whether they perform well or not, is because the Leader has low expectations about what people are capable of achieving. Where there are low expectations on what people can do, then what will happen is that such low expectations will be met, again a classic case of 'you get what you give'. Sometimes Leaders operate in the 'doesn't matter' style because they can't be bothered, sometimes in the mistaken belief of confusing abdication for delegation/empowerment, sometimes because they lack the assertiveness or will to deal with the situation.



One practical example of what can happen is when a new Leader is appointed to a team. In the early days the team will test out the new Leader, perhaps gently and subtly, perhaps more overtly. One of the members might, say, start finishing early. The other members will be watching – if that person 'gets away with it' then others will start to follow, if the person doesn't then the rest know where they stand.

The opposite to people feeling that it doesn't matter whether they perform well or not is, of course, when it does matter, and it is the approach and action of the Leader which makes the difference. We are not being punitive here when we talk of rewards and penalties, of *High Challenge-High Support*, rather we would argue that although it may seem comfortable at one level, and an easy life, the 'doesn't matter' situation is not a healthy or enviable one. To be without recognition is to be impoverished.

Effective Leader/Developers have zero tolerance for 'doesn't matter' induced poor performance. Zero Tolerance is part of the *Broken Window Theory*, increasingly being used as a demonstrably successful way to fight crime. The idea and philosophy is simple. If a broken window is not repaired, others are soon smashed, and before long the building is wrecked. The squalor encourages lawlessness and minor crime and, in due course, spawns more serious crime. If, on the other hand, the window is repaired, a positive environment is maintained and people are more likely to respect the law. It is all about dealing with problems in their infancy and not allowing them to escalate to become more major.

The feeling that it doesn't matter is, of course, the *Broken Window* of Leading and Developing High Performance. Let us be clear that we are not linking poor performance at work with criminality, rather pointing out that the *Broken Window* approach fits in the workplace too. The window is broken, in this sense if there is no recognition through Rewards and Penalties for good performance – it doesn't actually matter whether the person performs well or not. The approach in such cases is to find the right rewards and penalties, those which have a consequence to the person concerned, and to apply them consistently until they have sustained effect.



## 12. Does the person feel penalised for doing the right thing?

A Works Manager placed much stress on wanting his managers to take initiatives. When asked what happened when they did and got it right his reply was "Nothing, its their job". When asked what happened when they took an initiative and got it wrong, he replied "I tell them off" (or words to that effect). It transpired that his managers rarely, if ever, took initiatives – not surprisingly since they learned quickly that doing what was 'right' resulted never in reward, only in penalties.

When you have an inconvenient or unpleasant task to be done, who do you tend to give it to? The person who complains least or the one who complains most? If you consistently give such tasks to the person who complains least, then you are penalising that person for doing the 'right thing' of being co-operative and willing. Likewise, at home, which child receives the most attention? The one who creates the most fuss, or the one who is 'well behaved'? And will the latter start to feel penalised for doing the right thing and change their behaviour to get some attention?

Another example is that, until recently, in schools, girls tended to out-perform boys until their mid teens. At that age, penalties like 'It's not feminine to be a swat' or 'You'll be unattractive to boys' switched in, with the result that the girls tended, subsequently, to not out-perform the boys. More recently, perhaps because of changes in society, the previous 'penalties' have less affect, with the result that girls tend to continue to out-perform boys.

If the person does feel penalised for doing the right thing, then you must act to remove the penalties.

## 13. Are there good outcomes if the person does the wrong thing?

One obvious example is when an individual creates difficulties about taking on a task which then ends up elsewhere. A less obvious one perhaps, is where the reward comes from having a nickname or reputation for not performing – eg, "he's a real maverick". Another is staying within the security of a comfort zone rather than experiencing the discomfort of moving outside it, even though it is in both the individual's and the organisation's interest to take on a wider range of work.



Which of your people gets the most attention from you? Those who do the wrong thing or those who perform well? In mental institutions it was realised that patients who created the most disturbance got the most attention; it did not take long for other patients to realise that if they wanted attention they should act in the same way. Staff, too, learned that they needed to reward the good behaviour not just give attention to those doing the 'wrong' thing.

> *A group of 9 year-old children were on an outward bound type of experience. Halfway down a mountain, one little boy, less developed than the rest, soiled his pants. The staff were very attentive and reassuring to him. At the foot of the mountain, another one did the same and received the same kind of treatment. Then on the coach on the way home, another one did the same. Fortunately for the staff, at this stage, they realised what was happening!*

It is terribly easy to inadvertently reward the wrong thing. One large company needed to reduce staff numbers; they were very well intentioned and the redundancy terms it offered were particularly generous. It had four times the number of volunteers than it needed, which created a dilemma for the company. In the end they only allowed the poor performers to go (who got rewarded for doing the wrong thing?). The good performers, of course, felt penalised for doing the right thing, and learned very quickly that if they wanted to receive the same package next time round, they had better become poor performers. Absenteeism, lateness, quality, output deteriorated dramatically.

When the situation is one where there are good outcomes if the person does the wrong thing, then the Leader must change that situation by creating positive outcomes for good performance, and to include negative outcomes if the poor performance continues.

If the performance issue is a Won't Do one and does not result from what was described in steps 11, 12 or 13 (that is, the answers to the questions posed was NO), then there is one further possibility to consider.

## 14. Are there any job design features which get in the way of good performance?



For example, a secretary who is required to produce detailed, accurate typing of a manuscript and at the same time answer a constant stream of queries, despite having both high Can Do and Will Do, is unlikely to be able to get into the rhythm required.

Another example would be with air traffic controllers where the concentration required means that the job design, as well as the equipment and layout, has to be such to guarantee high performance.

There may be, in the situation, inappropriate equipment or poor job design which inhibit good performance. We are not talking about a perfect working environment here, but factors which are the root cause of poor performance, despite high Can Do and Will Do. These tend to happen rarely, but for both fairness and accurate diagnosis, they need to be considered.

The final question to be addressed, in the very rare case of a person who is still not performing to a satisfactory standard through lack of Will Do, is .......

## 15. Does the person have appropriate potential for this work?

If the Leader has faced the situation squarely, using *High Challenge-High Support*, acting with appropriate Positive Regard and, having diagnosed the root cause of the performance issue accurately, has followed through with vigour and resolution, then, in a very few cases, the person may not have appropriate potential for the particular work. This can be so even when it is not a Skill issue, but a Will or Attitude one. It may be that the particular problem has become so entrenched (possibly because it was not addressed previously), or is so deep-rooted that it is beyond the time and capability of the Leader to remedy.

In such a situation, High Challenge is again called for, where the Leader has to accept the Challenge that, having genuinely done all that s/he could do, it is time to resolve the situation and move on. In some circumstances this may mean invoking the formal disciplinary procedures, or redeployment to suitable work, or even dismissal. This may be painful and involve difficulties, but the alternative of not dealing with the situation and bringing it to resolution, is likely to be yet more painful in the long run.

It should only be the exceptional case which gets to this stage. The vast majority of performance issues are capable of being resolved, but only if the Leader/Developer is able to diagnose the root cause of the issue. S/he can then deal with the person, as a person, in the ways described in the following chapters.



The following Case Study illustrates this well, in addition to demonstrating how proper diagnosis is the starting point for resolving performance issues.

# Case Study

Jill Smith was the Accounts Controller for XYZ Ltd. Each month she had to collate data from some thirty or so Line Managers across a number of sites and include this data in a report for the Board.

The problem was that the Line Managers, over whom Jill had no direct authority, were inconsistent in providing the data on time. It was a simple task for them, but they were very busy people with many competing demands on their time, and often they did not give high priority to what Jill needed doing. This was creating a severe difficulty for Jill whose own report was often late, for which she was criticised. Moreover, she and her staff spent a great deal of time chasing up and giving reminders to Line Managers every month end, and also in persuading them that the task was important, and in reviewing the system to see whether it could be improved. Jill's staff were becoming demoralised and Jill knew that the Board members were beginning to doubt her competence. As a person she got on well generally with the Line Managers, and had sought their co-operation in getting their data in on time several times, but this only had a temporary effect.



## What Jill Did

She used the flow chart to analyse the performance issue. She decided that it was the lack of performance on the part of the Line Managers which prevented her from performing, and that the Undesirable Behaviours were that:

> *Line Managers did not provide the data specified consistently and reliably on time or to the required accuracy*

While the Desirable ones were for:

> ***Line Managers to consistently and reliably, and without being reminded each month, provide the required data on time and to the required accuracy***

Jill was also sure that they clearly knew what was expected, that they had the competence to do so, and that the problem was in the 'Won't Do' category. She decided, eventually, that the root cause of the issue was Step 11 of the flow chart, in that the Line Managers felt that it didn't matter whether they performed or not.

She considered asking one of the Directors whether to send the Line Managers a 'strong note', but rejected this idea as it made her appear and feel powerless, a victim in fact; also Jill realised that the effect of such a note would wear off over time and that she would be back to the old situation. Also, she rejected the idea of sending out reminders every month as the Line Managers were becoming dependent on this and, anyway, it was taking up too much of her time and that of her staff.

What Jill arranged to do was send out to the Board her report on time, even though she had to make estimates for the missing information, and to state in the report that it was incomplete because the necessary information had not been received from the Line Managers named. This created positive outcomes for those not named and negative outcomes for those named.



However, the most important and impressive part of what Jill did was not so much what she did, but HOW she did it. She hung on to her Positive Regard for the Line Managers who had caused her so much tribulation. So, after agreeing her approach with her Leader, she made a point of speaking to each Line Manager about the new system, followed this up in writing, including the start date of the new approach, and deliberately did not start the habit again of reminding them.

The first month, of course, some Line Managers were still late and were 'named' in the way described. The reaction was interesting; those who were 'named' were embarrassed but felt it was a 'fair cop' – after all they couldn't blame Jill, she had made a point of letting them know what was to happen, and the responsibility for not getting the data in was theirs. They felt OK about Jill, and didn't see her setting up a Win:Lose situation.

If, however, Jill had sprung the new situation on them without warning, setting them up to fail in fact, the late Line Managers would still probably have felt it was a 'fair cop', but one that was unfair in that it was set up to be a Win:Lose instead of a Win:Win. The problem with a Win:Lose, of course, is that somehow or other it gets turned into a Lose:Lose.

It would have been so easy for Jill to have resorted to 'war games' in the action she decided, particularly as the situation had given her some difficulties. Deciding the action, based on a good diagnosis, is not enough - it needs to be carried through with both Challenge and Support, with Positive Regard and Genuineness.

In the particular situation, the data was consistently provided, on time, after the first month. The solution endured.

# Chapter Summary

- *The first step in solving people performance problems is to diagnose the problem accurately.*
- *People aren't daft – they do things for a reason. They tend to do things they find rewarding and avoid doing things where there is a negative consequence or payoff for them.*
- *What gets rewarded gets done.*
  - *You get more of the behaviours you reward... and*
  - *It is easy to inadvertently reward the wrong thing*
- *People don't have to be ill to get better. In other words, the process applies to competent or good performers, who could do even better, as well as to currently poor performers.*
- *What is the performance issue? Define it for yourself in terms of Present Undesirable Behaviours and Future Desirable Behaviours. Be Explicit. Where there is a range of issues, start with one or two, don't try to solve them all at once.*
- *Does the person clearly know what is expected?*
  - *Do they have the skills and knowledge required, that is, is it a Can't Do issue?*
  - *Or could they do what is required if their life depended upon it, that is, is it a Won't Do issue?*
- *Most performance issues, once the person knows clearly what is expected, are 'Don't Want To' ones.*
- *Work through the flow chart systematically to identify the cause of the issue, and associated rewards and penalties.*
- *Decide a solution, act and follow up, then move on to the next issue.*
- *Build performance step by step.*

chapter 6

# Rewards and Penalties

- *How Rewards and Negative Consequences Shape Behaviour and Habits*
- *Rewards Available for the Leader/Developer to Use*
    - *Description of Rewards*
- *The Important Difference Between Extrinsic and Intrinsic Rewards*
- *The Reward of Recognition - Given Genuinely*
- *The Psychological Need for 'Stroking'*
- *Conditional and Unconditional Positive and Negative Strokes*
- *The Importance of Consistency*
- *Chapter Summary*



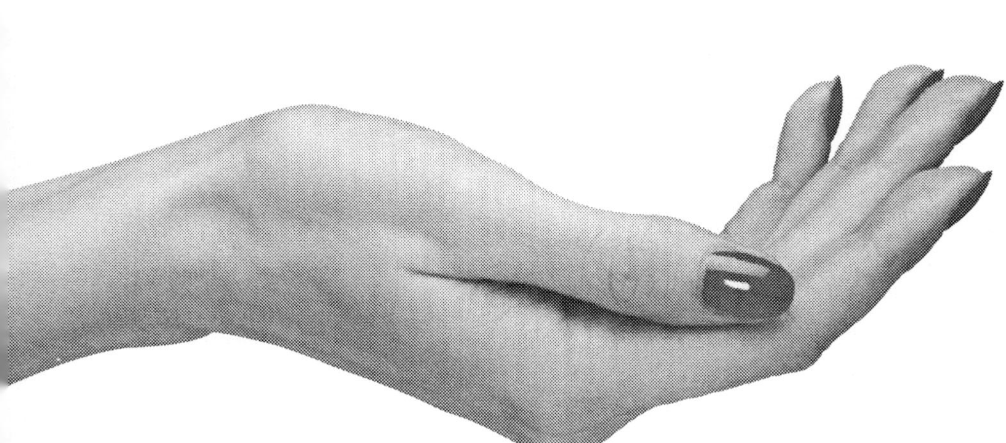

# How Rewards and Negative Consequences Shape Behaviour and Habits

> *In the early days of a now major electronics company, one of the founders was in his office working late when, without pausing to knock, in burst a research scientist shouting, "I've done it, I've done it!"*
>
> *The founder knew the importance of the project the scientist was working on and the effort that had gone into it. It was a moment of celebration; spontaneously he wanted to give the scientist something to show his appreciation and mark the moment. Pulling open his desk drawer all he could find was a banana. Speechlessly, because he could not find the right words to say, so great was the significance of the achievement to the fledgling company, he held out the banana for the scientist to take, both parties recognising immediately what it meant.*
>
> *The company now has the 'Golden Banana Award' where a small golden banana marks and celebrates occasions of high achievement.*



What **gets rewarded gets done**. What people find rewarding they tend to do more of, what they find unrewarding they tend to do less of, and the Leader/Developer can have much influence on both aspects of this. Rewards, and Penalties, shape behaviour and habits, cause people to perform well or not, to develop and grow. They are tangible expressions as to whether people are 'on course' or not, they let people know where they stand and how they are doing, they provide the context in which effort will be applied or withheld. In a Low Challenge-Low Support environment, for example, apathy and alienation will reign, in a *High Challenge-High Support* context there will be commitment and endeavour. Without appropriate rewards, particularly those where feedback is involved, people are working in a void; they are being asked to roller skate in the dark on the top of a tall building to use the analogy that was introduced in Chapter 1.

It is also terribly easy, inadvertently or otherwise, to reward the wrong thing, as was seen in Chapter 5 – Diagnosing Performance Issues. Organisations may, for example, proclaim the importance they place on team working, but if the appraisal system and other reward mechanisms do not reflect this, focusing on individual achievement only, then collaboration will not occur – internal competition will.

We are not talking here of Pavlovian dogs or what Hertzberg called 'Jumping for the Jelly Beans'. Rather the emphasis and intent is to facilitate and enable people to be successful in developing their abilities, performance and potential; or to grow from perhaps Dependency to Interdependence; or to be able to 'surf the wave of change' rather than being swamped by it. Giving appropriate rewards is not only a Transactional process based on improving day to day performance, but also a leadership-based Transitional one to achieve the vision of a person performing at their very best and achieving their full potential. The underlying ethos is to enable rather than to control.

Of course individuals will differ in their levels and types of motivation patterns, and in their experience and maturity in a job, which in turn will affect the kind of rewards that are most suitable. It's a case of 'different strokes for different folks'. Motivation and also Leadership Styles will be explained subsequently as an important way of fine tuning the approach.

If you asked a group of managers to brainstorm a list of rewards which are available to them to award, a typical list would be....

*Self Esteem and Worth*

*Interesting Work, Job Satisfaction, Bonuses, Fun*

*Responsibility and Trust*

*Favourite Work, Job Security, Belonging, Freedom*



*Teamwork*

*Good Appraisal, Personal Growth, Bigger Office*

*Recognition*

*Pension, Development, Company Car, Promotion, Praise*

*Time Off*

*Good Work, Well Done, Prizes, Money, Thank You*

*Pub*

*Doughnuts, Coffee*

*Cake*

... and when such rewards are examined more closely, their application and effect are typically seen to be as follows:

| | |
|---|---|
| **Money** | This is only effective if there is a strong and demonstrable link between performance and rewards. |
| **Promotion** | Leaders usually cannot offer a firm promise of promotion but they can help their people to perform well and highly to improve their chances, and champion their cause. |
| **Security** | Security comes from being employable and flexible, that is performing capably and being able to cope with change. |
| **Recognition** | Praise, increased responsibility, trust, 'well done', letters of congratulation, freedom and many more are all forms of recognition, as are the symbolic one of giving cakes, coffee, bananas etc. |
| **Time Off** | Accommodating requests from good performers (but not poor ones) or 'job and finish' are examples of rewards. |
| **Fun** | Making work zestful, developing team spirit, celebrating achievements, competitions – creating enjoyment so that people want to pull out the stops and show what they can do. |
| **Learning & Personal Growth** | Being challenged, learning new skills, developing experience. |
| **Interesting or Favourite Work** | Allocation of such work to high performers as a reward. |
| **Ownership & Responsibility & Delegation** | Trusting good performers by making the job 'theirs'. |
| **Job Satisfaction** | By creating meaning to the work and developing personal mastery to do it well. |
| **Self Esteem & Worth** | Through creating and reinforcing actual competence and contribution. |

## The Important Difference Between Extrinsic and Intrinsic Rewards

When such a typical list is examined more closely, it is apparent that some of the rewards are extrinsic, that is, provided by an 'outside' stimulus, such as money, larger office or a new car. Others are intrinsic – psychological rewards experienced directly by the individual. So, some rewards are from the outside, while others harmonise with, and facilitate what is already important for the person; they connect with what is there. It is these latter rewards which can have the greatest and most long-term effect.

This is not to discount the importance of money and other extrinsic factors. The level of material reward has to be reasonably right, otherwise the relationship won't be seen as a fair one. However, there are a number of disadvantages with relying on material rewards only, especially money. It can become like Dane gold where, in the days of the Vikings, the English Kings bribed the Danes not to trouble them. It worked, but the problem was the price went up year by year until the Treasury was exhausted, then the Danes invaded anyway. Relying on material rewards is a one way, losing bet, in the sense that all behaviour ends up having a price.



There is another, compelling, reason why reliance cannot be placed on material rewards solely. This is because they lie in the province of the organisation, not the individual Leader. Salary scales, promotion systems, pension schemes, car policies are controlled by the organisation; a team member has access to them by right as s/he is a member of the organisation. To put it crudely, once a team member is in the organisation, the same benefits will broadly apply to all the members of the team except, exceptionally, where extremely low performance carries the risk of discipline or even termination, and very high performance gives the possibility of increased reward. For the majority though, broadly speaking, the same extrinsic rewards will apply.

Of course, the Leader may be able to influence promotion, bonuses (if they apply) and performance related pay where it is used. What is important, in performance related pay terms, is that it is not the amount of differential award (often quite small relative to the whole) which creates the effect, but the recognition involved. The Leader too, has an influence on material rewards in arguably a more important and less obvious way, that is to help team members guarantee their security through the security of employability, which in turn requires the habits of high performance, flexibility and the ability to learn and cope with change.

A uni-dimensional reliance, by the Leader, on material rewards is not a good idea, providing the level of such rewards is reasonable in the first place. If the rewards available to the Leader to give are allocated across a scale, typically the scale would look something like this:

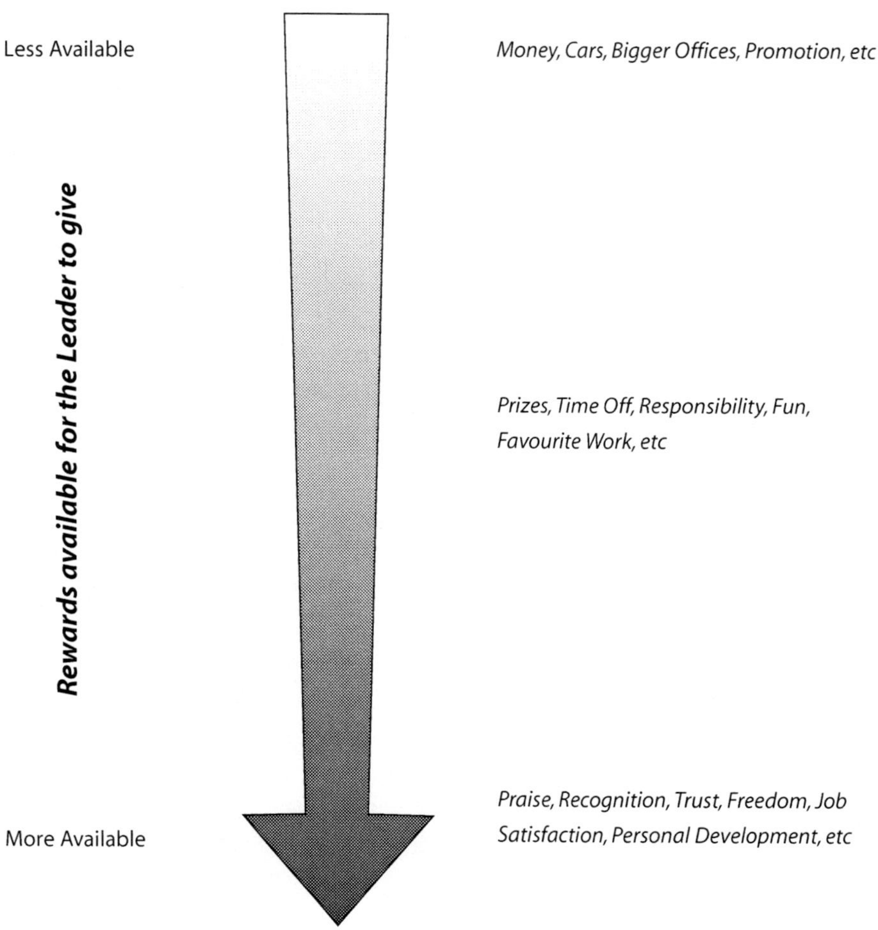

# The Reward of Recognition – Given Genuinely

The set of rewards most available to effective Leaders, and the ones effective Leaders use most, are those such as praise, recognition, responsibility, trust etc. There is a fortunate coincidence and paradox here; not only are such rewards – and penalties through the withholding of them – the most available to the Leader, they are also the most powerful. Research study after research study has demonstrated that recognition consistently appears at the top, or close to the top, of people's requirements from work.

Praise, responsibility, trust and many other rewards are, essentially, to do with recognition. But – and it's an important BUT – that recognition has to be genuine and authentic, and underpinned by the mindset of *High Challenge-High Support*, where there is both strong commitment to the person and a preparedness to give not just praise when due but also to face and deal with inappropriate performance.



With many Leaders it is as though they erect a glass screen between themselves and their team, they use 'management speech' which blurs the message and the relationship. What they say has little impact or meaning because it's not from them as a person, it's from them in their role of Leader – *"they would say that wouldn't they".* Equally some Leaders try to get so friendly with their team that they lose the ability to reprimand, a mistake often made by newly appointed Leaders, especially when assigned to lead a team in which they were previously a member.

The greatest reward you have to give is **yourself**. When you see something exceptional, when you see one of your people make an important step forward, when you see extra effort applied to overcome a problem, you will be delighted and will say so. The other person is there, s/he matters. Nelson Mandela tells in his biography how, after many years in prison and when his spirits were at their lowest, an unseen voice from a new guard said through the cell grill, "I *see you Nelson Mandela, and I respect you*", and the powerful restorative affect that statement had on him.

The opposite also applies. When the task is done in a slipshod manner, when customers don't get the attention they deserve, when problems are hidden or disguised, it will matter to you and you will express your disappointment, clearly and directly.

# The Psychological Need for 'Stroking'

Why is it that recognition is such an important need for the majority of us? In the language of Transactional Analysis (a psychological model which describes what happens between people, and why we often behave the way we do), such recognition is called 'Strokes', or 'Stroking'. People need Strokes to maintain their physical and psychological well being.

For example, it is well established that babies and infants need physical contact (Stroking) of a positive, nurturing nature, to emotionally grow and prosper. There is evidence too, and more surprisingly, that lack of such Stroking impairs the physical growth and well being of the child.

As people move from childhood to adulthood, their need for Strokes continues, as does the need for recognition. The strength of this need in us is such that some people, in the absence of positive recognition, will contrive to seek 'put downs' and 'Negative Strokes', which are at least a form of recognition, and which are better than not being recognised at all. There is an African greeting, "*I see you*", which well illustrates the importance of recognition.



What happens in our society is that at a certain stage into adulthood, it becomes no longer culturally acceptable to Stroke people physically, such as by caressing them or with other physical contact – or indeed to be Stroked by them (except with the closest of relationships). Instead we begin to use other forms of recognition, such as words, smiles, gestures, frowns, nods etc.

A Positive Stroke is one which carries a "*You're OK*" message and usually results in the recipient feeling good and reaffirmed. A Negative Stroke results in unpleasant feelings. How Strokes are given or received tends to reflect the life position in the OK Corral (shown in Chapter 2) that a person is in. People who feel OK about themselves and others tend to seek out exchanges of Positive Strokes; those who feel others are not OK tend to give Negative Strokes, and those who feel "*I'm not OK*" tend to seek out Negative Strokes which will increase their not *OK* feelings.

The rule seems to be that Negative Strokes are better than no Strokes at all, although it is the Positive Strokes which nourish us. One fairly extreme case we came across graphically illustrated this.

*A small team of five people were supervised by a team leader, who had a strong friendship with one member of the team, which was made apparent to all the others by obvious strokes about how much the team leader enjoyed his company.*

*Another member of team didn't share the same social relationship with the team leader but did receive frequent pats on the back for the quality of her work. The third member of the team also received feedback but it tended to be more critical, while the fourth member was the butt of some fairly personal put-downs from the team leader. All were receiving the same contact with their leader and accepted it as normal.*



*It was the fifth member who experienced the most difficulty – he was ignored by the leader, excluded, often inadvertently, from briefings and who asked for a transfer to another team after only 6 weeks.*

Such is the power of recognition that some people have learned, through their life experiences, that they would rather be recognised through Negative Strokes than ignored, and play the psychological game of "*Kick me*", where they set themselves up to be 'kicked'. It does, at least, result in some form of acknowledgement.

# Conditional and Unconditional Positive and Negative Strokes

Strokes may be Conditional *(for doing)* or Unconditional *(for being)* as follows:

| | | |
|---|---|---|
| POSITIVE | CONDITIONAL | eg: *"That was a good report you produced; it was clear, concise and summed up the issues"* |
| POSITIVE | UNCONDITIONAL | eg: *"I like you, you're a good bloke"* |
| NEGATIVE | CONDITIONAL | eg: *"When someone has an idea you always criticise it right away, so people are reluctant to make suggestions. Next time someone has one, find something positive to say about it first, before pointing out the flaws"* |
| NEGATIVE | UNCONDITIONAL | eg: *"You're a waste of space"* |



Generally, Positive Unconditional Strokes are more suited to the home or social life than to the workplace, while Negative Unconditional ones have limited or no value anywhere. If we look at Conditional and Unconditional Strokes as a form of recognition in terms of the Onion Model, we can see that Negative Unconditional Strokes will be experienced as attacking the core integral self and will provoke the kind of reaction they deserve. Unconditional Positive Strokes, although very nourishing, do not change workplace behaviour. Conditional Strokes though, influence Behaviour and, importantly, Attitudes – for example, through praise and recognition when good performance is achieved, and through Negative ones (reprimands) when it is not.

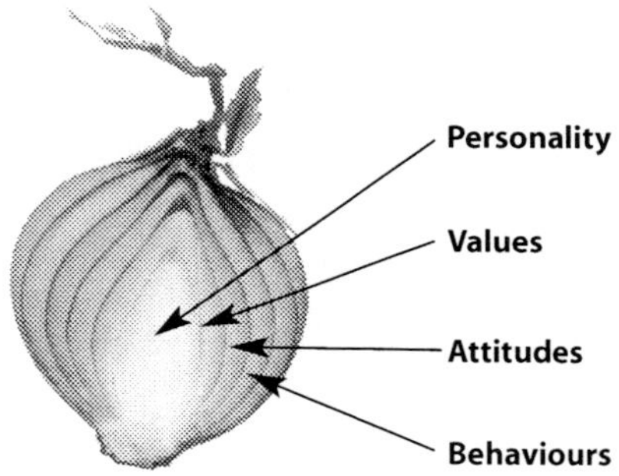

What, too, is critically important in all this is, once again, the underlying attitude or mindset of I+U+. There is all the difference in the world in seeing the other person as basically OK, that is, as having fundamental worth and value, and with Positive Regard, even though what they did on this occasion (their Behaviour) was not appropriate. It is not the person who is not OK, but their Behaviour. It is when this mindset is present that a Negative Conditional Stroke will be received and most usually accepted.

In the Stroking Exercise involving five volunteers, described a little earlier, what also comes out clearly is that it is legitimate to give authentic Negative Conditional Strokes (or reprimands), and they will be received as long as they come from a I+U+ viewpoint. Then they become feedback, not personal attack. When Negative Strokes, Conditional or Unconditional, come from an I+U- position, the U-recipient will resist or resent being viewed this way, and also feel aggressed upon if the Negative Stroke was an Unconditional one. Further if you stay in the I+U+ mindset, even if you, yourself are being aggressed upon, or when the other person is operating from I-U+, then the chances are that, in both cases, they will eventually shift to an I+U+ dialogue with you.

# The Importance of Consistency

What also matters is the crucial Leadership characteristic of consistency. A good example of this, or lack of it and its consequences, is given in the following description of Captain Bligh of 'Mutiny on the Bounty' fame. Bligh was, in fact, a brilliant Leader, but only in special circumstances. The fatal flaw he had as a Leader was his lack of consistency.

> *"There were a number of things about him that were already causing a measure of uneasiness – the uncertain nature of his moodiness, the way he would nag, nag, nag away on some failure, real or supposed, large or small, one day, then ignore some serious piece of mismanagement the next day. There wasn't any consistency about the man."*

Captain Bligh and Mr Christian – Richard Hough



Praise is part of recognition but it is not necessarily the kind of recognition we are talking about. There was a scene in the TV sitcom series 'Are You Being Served', where old Mr Grace, supported by a very attractive nurse, would get out of the lift and say to the assembled staff, "You're all doing very well", then disappear back into the lift, leaving the staff completely 'under-whelmed' by the blandness of the ritual.

Generalised praise, particularly when it is not genuine but a ritual, is not very helpful and can be patronising. Praise and thanks as part of everyday courtesy is something else again. But what we are talking about here is recognition for a specific action or piece of behaviour to encourage more of the same, which is much more than an everyday courtesy. Such recognition can be verbal or non verbal (as in the Banana story but, say, with a cup of coffee), and symbolic or tangible. It marks and celebrates what has been achieved in the step forward.

We are not just talking about major achievements here, but any significant move in the direction you want the person to take. Change is a series of small steps, each one reinforced on a little and often basis. Equally, as well as rewards, the use of consequences or penalties reinforces this process. However all the evidence is that rewards work better than penalties, that it is positive reinforcement through recognition which has the greatest effect. The cardinal rule is to...

***Catch someone doing something right !***

Rather than the more usual...

## *Ignoring what is going well and blitzing what is going wrong*

...and, with feet firmly on the ground and being realistic, to adopt the 'Catch Someone Doing Something Right' approach as a way of life, while being prepared also to confront and deal with negative behaviour by penalties or consequences, as well as future rewards.

As was said in the Chapter 5 – Diagnosing Performance Issues - people aren't daft, they do things for a reason, and the reasons are the awards they obtain or the consequences they avoid. It is the doing of things, that is Behaviour, that Leaders who develop high performance concentrate on, so the right thing gets done. When the right things get done, consistently, Attitudes are also likely to shift, which in turn consolidates and underpins the Behaviour.



Once a performance issue has been accurately diagnosed then the rewards, and avoidance of penalties, the individual is presently getting can be seen, and the Leader/Developer can then substitute more appropriate ones. Such rewards and penalties most often will not be large in scale, but what is certain is that they will need to come from the Leader him/herself, and be well delivered. How they are delivered will be the subject of the Chapter 7 – Maximising People's Potential Through Feedback. Of course individuals vary as to what matters to them. so we will also need to look at individual motivation styles (Chapter 8) and also take into account where the person is on their development cycle so we can adjust our style accordingly (Chapter 9).

# Chapter Summary

- *People do things for a reason, consciously or subconsciously*
- *The reasons are the rewards they receive or penalties they avoid*
- *High Performance is developed through a little and often approach of appropriate rewards and penalties*
- *The greatest source of rewards a Leader has to offer are to do with Recognition in its various forms*
- *Effective recognition is Conditional – that is, it is specific to what has been done, such as an improvement made*
- *The biggest reward the Leader has to offer is him/herself, in the sense that it is clearly seen by the received that the reward matters to the Leader*
- *Recognition is a form of 'Stroking', an important need and part of the human condition*
- *Rewards and Reprimands only work well when they are authentic and come from an I+U+ position*
- *Positive reinforcement works better than negative reinforcement*
- *'Catch Someone Doing Something Right' – look for it*
- *Tailor rewards and penalties to fit the individual*

chapter 7

# Maximising People's Potential Through Feedback

## Catch them doing it right


- *The Importance of Performance Development Feedback*
- *Feedback and Rewards*
- *The Flight Plan Analogy*
- *Catching People Doing Something Right*
- *Giving Clear, Assertive Feedback*
- *The Skills of Giving Positive Feedback*
  - *Why People Sometimes Don't Hear Praise*
- *The Skills of Giving Negative Feedback*
  - *The Difference Between Technical Feedback and Reprimands*
  - *Why People Sometimes Don't Hear Reprimands*
- *Dealing with Negative Reactions*
- *Chapter Summary*


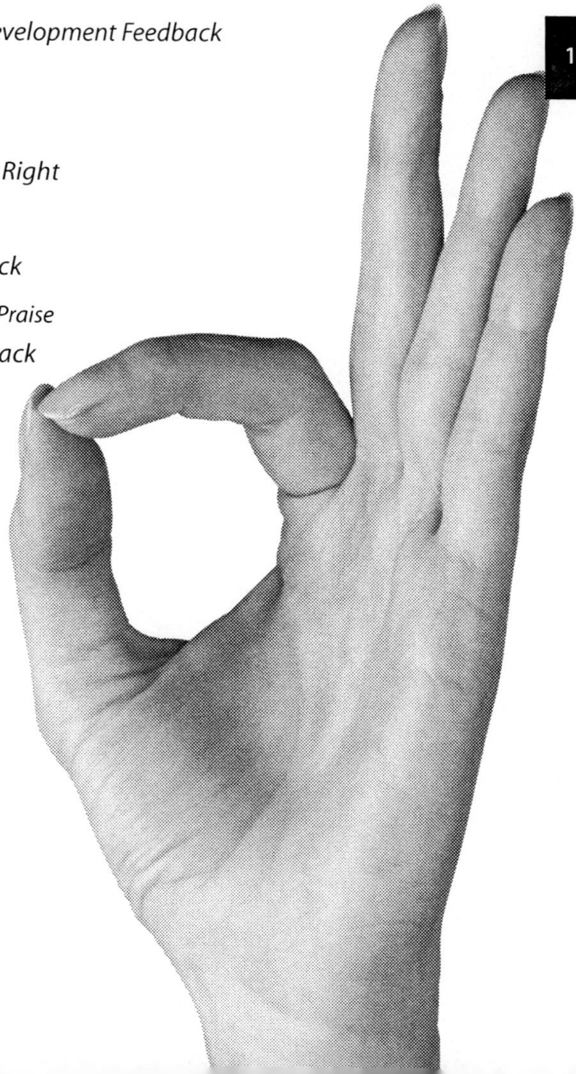

# The Importance of Performance Development Feedback

Feedback allows people to know whether they are on course or not, where they are, how they are doing. It is a crucial part of the navigation system for continuous improvement, but the feedback is only useful if it is explicit, relevant, focuses on behaviour and, above all, is heard.

In the context of Performance Development, feedback is given for the purpose of encouraging someone to do more (or less of) the same. When reinforced with the right rewards or consequences it guides and shapes efficient performance, and encourages growth, personal mastery and success. This is so whether correcting present poor performance, helping someone through the transition curve of change, coaching and mentoring someone from Dependency to Interdependence, or conducting an enabling appraisal. Feedback provides personal security, reassurance and certainty in an often otherwise turbulent and confusing world. It allows people to know:



- *where they stand*
- *what is expected of them*
- *how they are performing*
- *how they are progressing*

and, as a consequence of the feedback, it makes it easier for people to take increasing responsibility for developing themselves and becoming the best they can be.

An example of the power of simple, explicit and continual feedback is shown in this short real-life situation:

*A consultant had to make a presentation to a group he did not know in a venue deep in the heart of some countryside with which he was unfamiliar. There was very little space in his schedule to get there on time. Despite his experience in giving such presentations a degree of anxiety was around; the presentation was important for his partners and himself and the journey would be a long and arduous one.*

*The directions to find the venue provided by the hotel were excellent. It said things like, "You will see a large station on your right, the sign to XYZ you are looking for is a few hundred yards past this on the left," and "once you have passed the Mucky Duck pub, on your left, start looking for a fork, and take the right fork."*

*The point of the story is that the directions provided continual feedback so that the driver, in unfamiliar territory and doing something new, knew how he was doing and that he was on track in his search for the conference venue. They allowed him to get to his destination efficiently and on time. Importantly, they had the effect of removing, from the situation, anxiety and stress that otherwise would have been present.*

*In this case the directions, and their explicitness and feedback as part of them, were enabling as they facilitated successful performance.*

# Feedback and Rewards

Feedback, on its own, can be a powerful reward, as it is an experience of Recognition and Praise which is relevant, real and centred. If used well, it will build self esteem, self confidence and trust, and enlarge the horizons for greater success. It reinforces the possible. This applies even when the feedback is negative, provided that again it is well delivered, it is conditional (ie relates to Behaviour rather than Values or Personality), and it is known by the recipient that praise is also given when due. Giving feedback, face to face, is a 'moment of truth', the communication process through which Leader/Developers – having diagnosed a performance issue, having decided in explicit terms what behaviours are and are not required, having thought about appropriate rewards and consequences – put it all into action.



> *Those Leaders who are committed and skilled in developing high performance do not act at random. Rather they have a purpose, an underlying vision, which sees each team member performing at their very best, fulfilling their whole potential. They have this vision in their minds eye continuously, seeing each step along the journey is completed by a series of small steps, each one dependent on the previous one, and that real change comes about by the cumulative effect and reinforcement of all these small steps. They operate by a little and often principle, knowing that usually it is unrealistic to achieve sustained 'big bang' type change, but that a consolidated series of incremental improvements is the way forward. They start with the end (their vision) in mind, and they have planned the journey.*

# The Flight Plan Analogy

Giving Feedback is rather analogous to flying. For instance, if you turn up at Heathrow expecting to be flown to Acapulco you will have a quite reasonable expectation that the pilot will land at the right airfield, will have enough fuel and will generally get you there safely. You expect a competent professional, able to deal appropriately with any incident or deviation en route. In particular, you will expect the pilot to know where s/he is – their position – all the time, so that if the plane is off course, this can be corrected and the plane brought back on track. Equally, it is rare that the course will be a completely straight one, both because of navigational hazards or other difficulties.

What pilots do of course, is to construct a flight plan. They don't expect to take off from Heathrow and worry about how they are going to get to their destinations later (hopefully). So it is with effective Leaders who successfully develop High Performance.



These days aircrew can locate their position through global positioning electronic systems which give them constant feedback that they are on course. In fact, an alarm will activate if they are not. They are still required to fly over position beacons occasionally, which give an alternative, yet more certain position of where they are.

In the 'flight plan' of the Leader of High Performance, their beacons are appraisal meetings, often formal. But one absolute difference between effective Leaders and less effective ones, is that the effective ones do not wait and store up feedback for regular appraisal reviews (the beacons) perhaps once or twice a year, instead they give instant feedback continuously, hour by hour where necessary, day by day, week by week. If they see **someone doing something right** they say so, at the time, immediately; if a mistake is being made, or poor performance is observed, they deal with it there and then, rather than waiting for it to become a habit.

They are always on the lookout for good performance continuously, and catch and reinforce it immediately, for they know that positive reinforcement is much more effective than criticism.

## 'Flight Plan' Diagram

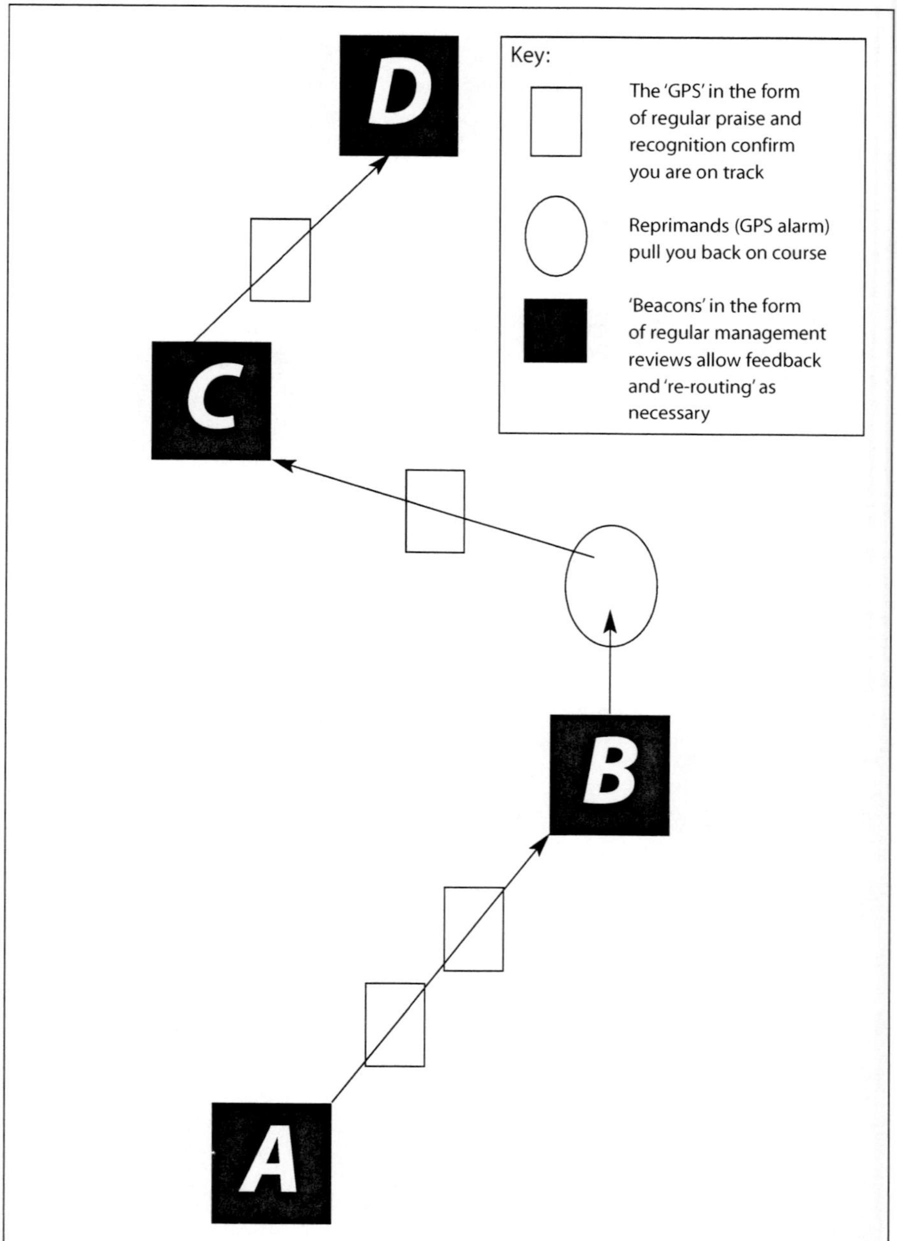

# Catch People Doing Something Right

We need to define what we mean by 'catching someone doing something right'. What we mean is an improvement, a step in the right direction, something different. Of course, someone who performs reliably and consistently deserves thanks and appreciation. But to concentrate on giving praise for basic things, like attendance at team meetings, debases the currency of feedback.

Maintaining someone's already High Performance requires, of course – and deserves – appropriate and authentic recognition, beyond the normal courtesies. However, an improvement, a step in the right direction, is something else and requires to be caught, celebrated and positively reinforced. This is what is meant by the phrase 'Catch Someone Doing Something Right'. You then encourage the next step, and 'catch that being done right' also. It doesn't matter how small these steps are, initially they are likely to be quite small as in the case when someone is caught up in the log jam of established habits and practices. When they reach a landing, so to speak, between the steps, then that is the time to consolidate the achievement by additional praise and recognition. Beware though of repeatedly praising the completion of an individual step, because the message then becomes one of reinforcing the person to stay where s/he is, and not to move on to the next stage. It is a continuous journey, for true excellence is an always moving state.



## The Pigeon Analogy

*In the field of research, animals are often trained to perform certain tasks. For example, pigeons have been trained to ring a bell. It was more than a million to one chance that they would succeed in ringing the bell without assistance. The first step in their training was to get them to move towards the bell. When they did move a step towards it they were rewarded with a grain of corn. If they had been stuffed full of corn at this stage, they would have stayed where they were, after all the reward is of a scale to reinforce them to do this. It was a further step, then a further, which got rewarded with more grains, and when the bell was rung the reward was special and treated as such.*

We are not suggesting here that people are in any way like pigeons. But the example of a series of small, attainable steps towards a goal, each one reinforced with feedback and recognition (not in the form of corn!) is apt, particularly during the Transactional stage of Mobilising. When people are equipped with the basic skills and, more importantly, have or have developed the will to move further, then a different type of learning applies. It moves from 'push' to 'pull', with the individual largely managing the learning themselves in partnership with the Leader/Developer. These are the Developing and Enabling stages of the process, with the Leader/Developer using Transformational skills to help this transition and then support people through this part of the process.

Although the Mobilising stage may involve much direction, the end game is to cause and help the person to be self-directing in their own continual performance improvement and learning, through, where necessary, equipping them with the building blocks – will, desire, competence – to do so.



Developers of High Performance then provide feedback regularly and as soon as they 'catch people doing something right'. Whilst they also let people know when things are not going right, they are particularly on the lookout for the former. They have high expectations about their peoples' performance, have a Vision (Flight Plan) about people performing at their very best, and are consistent. Their people know where they stand in that if they do good work it will be noticed and dealt with. Feedback becomes a way of life, people know in advance what to expect. In fact, the Leader will describe to new members of the team how they will be receiving strong feedback regularly in order to help them. In this way, while negative feedback is given, it won't be experienced as though it were a jet fighter screaming out of the sun. People will know the rules of engagement; positive and negative feedback given where due. So, on these occasions when negative feedback is appropriate, it will be heard and responded to more.

We are back to mindsets. The Leader who develops High Performance is not only skilled at giving feedback, it matters to him/her that the other person succeeds, and cares enough to give such feedback clearly and directly, both positive and negative. This in turn requires the skills and characteristics of Assertion, which we will deal with now before going on to look at the skills and techniques of Giving Effective Feedback.

# Giving Clear, Assertive Feedback

| M2: | Maintains Own Assertiveness | *Applying appropriately the underlying skills and attitudes of assertiveness, necessary for being explicit and giving feedback, but also to maintain consistency of standards and approach; exerting strong leadership, when necessary, to prevent the team from going in different directions* |
|---|---|---|

Our experience is that 'clear' Assertion is frequently one of the least developed sets of characteristics and skills needed for Developing High Performance. It is, however, the influencing style which underpins the giving of feedback, especially negative feedback, and it is also needed to support the High Challenge part of the *High Challenge-High Support* mindset. Majoring on High Support is not enough, in many situations, it is the combined approach which will more often cause movement forward. There are other influencing styles that the Leader/Developer of High Performance needs to have in his/her repertoire, but Assertion is the keystone of the set.

The culture of some environments seems to be almost entirely based on logical persuasion – a kind of debate to persuade, based on logic and the rationality of a point of view. In many performance issues this does not work very well, and degenerates into arguments and diversions, whereas an Assertion based approach is more likely to succeed. Then again being Non-Assertive means issues are not confronted and dealt with, leaving people in a void of not knowing where they stand, or praise is not given, at least not given well, as it requires Assertion to do this.

For some Leaders, part of the difficulty is that they confuse Assertion with Aggression, or feel Assertion is being too pushy. It isn't.

# ASSERTION

**AGGREGESSIVE** ←——— **ASSERTIVE** ———→ **NON-ASSERTIVE**

| | |
|---|---|
| **AGGRESSIVE** | Standing up for oneself and one's rights in a way that the rights of others are violated in the process<br><br>The middle of the 'Onion' is attacked<br>**[I Win – You Lose]** |
| **ASSERTIVE** | Standing up for oneself and one's rights in such a way that the other person's rights are not violated<br><br>Only the outer rings of 'Behaviour' and 'Attitudes' are addressed<br>**[I Win – You Win]** |
| **NON-ASSERTIVE** | To fail to stand up for oneself and one's rights effectively<br><br>**[You Win – I Lose]** |

When Leaders, who are confused by the difference, are encouraged to be strongly Assertive, the recipient's experience is usually one of surprise that the interaction was thought to be anywhere near Aggression. In fact, what is most likely to happen with non-Assertive Leaders is that, at some stage, they flip from being non-Assertive to Aggressive when their 'doormat' bank is full. Clearly this, with its consequences, is something to avoid.

What is more advantageous is to build up the Personal Power of Assertion, so that there is plenty in reserve when difficult situations have to be dealt with. In some ways it is analogous to what often happens when people develop martial arts – confidence grows, and shows, so that the more capable someone is the less likely they are to have to use such skills, and when they do it is all well under control.

> *"My definition of support would include respecting someone (sometimes oneself) enough to 'tell the truth' if necessary. I find this kind of support more difficult; it's easier to cop out. But it feels much more authentic to be honest. One small but memorable example from my own past experience concerned a man who was about to join me, from another team, to work on a new project. I was aware that he came to work late, went home early and spent much of the time he was in completing The Telegraph crossword. After a lot of thought I knew it was only fair for me to be up front about what I expected as team leader. He was 55 and I was young enough to be his daughter, but, scared as I was, I confronted him. To my astonishment he said 'No problem. No-one has ever even noticed my timekeeping before. I won't let you down.' And he didn't; he worked hard and was much happier for it. A valuable lesson for us both I believe."*

One other way of looking at it is back to the OK Corral, thus:

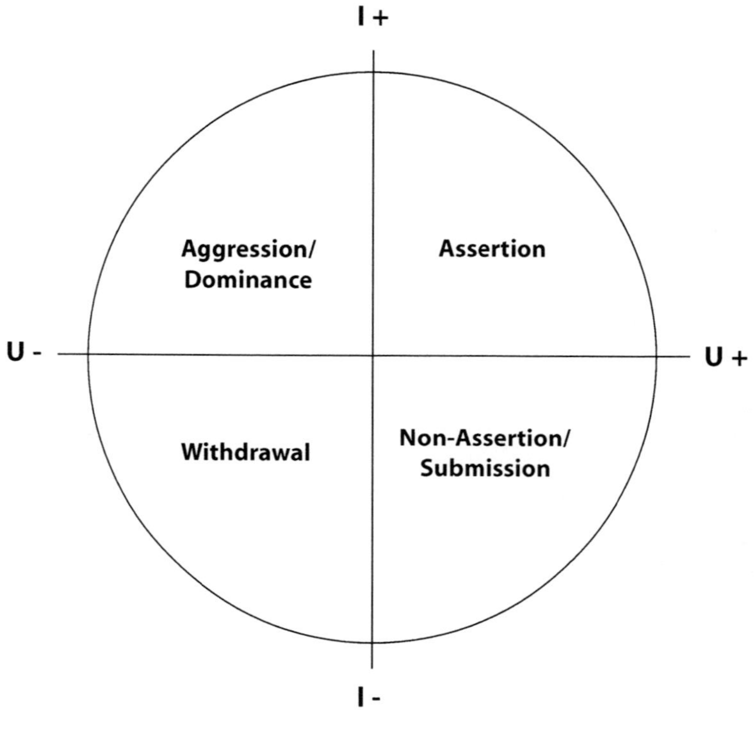


Assertion is based on the I+ U+ position, a dialogue between two mature adults, as it were, both capable of accepting responsibility for their actions, both OK people with Rights which need to be respected. Part of the Rights of the other person is to be treated as fundamentally OK (Personality and Values), even though their Behaviour or Attitude may not have been OK on this occasion. Again, part of these Rights include being praised and recognised for what has been achieved when it is real and significant (U+), not patronised or manipulated from a U- one (disguised or transparent). The Rights of the Leader include the absolute requirement to develop High Performance in the team and to tell people when they are not delivering.

Staying in the I+U+ position is desperately important when giving feedback, it's an all purpose ground rule which is the key to handling all kinds of situations, including difficult and contentious ones.

Being Assertive requires two specific ways of thinking (which we have just explored) and some simple skills. The essence of Assertion is expressed as follows:

**Assertiveness Mindset:**

| | |
|---|---|
| Stay in the I+ U+ Position | *If this is difficult, hang on to your Positive Regard and don't get 'hooked' into aggression, allowing yourself to be aggressed upon or dealing with the other person like a child. If you stay I+U+ the probability is that the other person will eventually respond in the same way.* |
| Look after Your Rights, and the Rights of the Other Person | *You have legitimate Rights, such as being respected as an individual, being treated with courtesy, having a point of view, asking for what you want, to be human and make a mistake, being listened to – so does the other person. Don't trample the other person's Rights.* |



**Assertiveness Skills & Behaviours:**

| | |
|---|---|
| Use the 'I' statement | *Not 'one', 'we', 'they', 'the company', 'my boss', 'the organisation', 'the rules' – but 'I'. Hiding behind other people dilutes the power of its message; this is from* ***you****. Remember the greatest reward you have to give is yourself – what is said has to come from you directly and you have to own it, whether it is praise or reprimand.* |

| | |
|---|---|
| Keep it Short and Succinct – Cut the Waffle | *Be direct and clear in saying what you want and need. Come to the point quickly and don't confuse the other person with a mass of verbiage or camouflage – just say what is on your mind and don't dress it up.* |
| Avoid Qualifiers | *Qualifiers like 'perhaps', 'may be', 'a little', 'if you wouldn't mind', etc, fog and weaken the message, and get in the way. Again, keep it short and succinct.* |
| Express Your Feelings | *"I'm angry that"... "I'm pleased that"... "I'm desperate that"... "I'm worried that"... "I'm delighted that"...*<br><br>*The power of the praise or reprimand comes from you; if it is authentic then feelings will show. This is not to say that you should lose your temper, shout or kiss the other person; but do let them know how you feel about what has happened. (In this we differ from many other writers on Assertion, where feelings do not enter the equation. Assertion without humanity can be experienced as an impersonal routine and result in a resistance of its own making.)* |
| Avoid Irritators | *Sarcasm or stings/tweaks like "I want you to do this... if you are capable of doing it", leak from a fundamentally I+U- position. Keep the assertion clean and uncontaminated.* |
| Use Appropriate Body Language | *Look at the other person, be there, relax, use an even tone of voice and, on occasions count to ten and take a deep breath. Stay in I+U+.* |

As has been said, Assertiveness is what underpins the giving of Effective Feedback. This is perhaps more obvious with the giving of negative feedback, but is necessary, too, with the giving of positive feedback. Experience of participants on training programmes shows that when they are asked to give some praise to someone else, what happens, frequently, is that the praiser does not look at the person being praised, a joke is made of it to cover embarrassment, often the praise has a 'put down' quality, and does not address a real issue. Many of us are not very good at giving praise. Yet, when a genuine piece of praise is well given, the affect on the person receiving it is striking.

A concern that people who are reluctant to use Assertion often have is they feel they might be discourteous (as well as being experienced as aggressive, as referred to earlier). To lay things out clearly and simply is not being discourteous (in our culture at least) it is clarifying, helpful and respectful.



One final Assertion technique which Leaders can find useful when dealing with people who are adroit at avoiding personal responsibility for what has happened, fudging issues or deflecting them away from the point, is called *Broken Record*.

What this involves is simply sticking to the point and not allowing yourself to be deflected, doing so by repeating what you want until the message is heard (hence the name Broken Record). An example of this would be:

**Leader:**

> *"In future, I want you to write down what actions we agree that you should take following our weekly meetings."*

**Team Member:**

> *"I don't need to write them down, I can remember."*

**Leader:**

> *"I understand that... but I want you to write them down so they don't get missed."*

**Team Member:**

> *"Why do I have to do it when no-one else is?"*

**Leader:**

*"We are not discussing anyone else now – I want you to write down the agreed actions."*

**Team Member:**

*"What difference will that make?"*

**Leader:**

*"I want you to write them down so you don't forget them."*

**Team Member:**

*"OK."*



Note how the Leader kept to the point of what s/he required and did not allow him/herself to be side-tracked into other avenues. Without being rude s/he did not allow him/herself to be fobbed off thus giving extra strength to the point being made.

*Broken Record* is very difficult to resist but, again, staying in the I+U+ mode is crucial.

# The Skills of Giving Positive Feedback

We can now move onto the skills of Giving Feedback, in a way which:

- *is assertively powerful and 'natural'*
- *focuses on Behaviour (and not Personality or Values)*
- *is part and parcel of everyday working life*
- *takes a short time to do*
- *is a crucial way of helping people to improve and develop, and to be recognised and rewarded*

**Positive Feedback – through Praise and Recognition**

**CATCH PEOPLE DOING SOMETHING RIGHT !**



- *Let people know, in advance, that you will be giving plenty of feedback*
- *Catch* ***improved*** *performance immediately – 10 seconds of* ***immediate*** *praise will reinforce the action much more effectively than a comment a week later at a formal review meeting*
- *Describe the good performance explicitly and its consequences, directly expressing your feelings*
- *Pause to allow the good feelings to sink in – the pause will also show them there is no 'sting in the tail'*
- *Encourage them to do more of the same*

Sometimes, though, when praise is used for the first time, or people have had a different experience of it in the past when it was not always used genuinely, they sometimes don't always 'hear' it. Should this happen, then it is useful to understand the reasons, so it can be better dealt with.

# Why People Sometimes Don't Hear Praise

- ***Waiting for the 'YES BUT'***

  *Many of us have been conditioned to being 'patted' as a prelude to being 'kicked', or have impending criticism introduced by some praise to sweeten the pill.*

  - *Keep the praise clear and uncontaminated*
  - *Repeat the praise if necessary*
  - *Make it clear when you want to deal with criticism and keep it separate*

- ***Embarrassment***

  *Sometimes people get embarrassed by praise, especially when they are not used to receiving it. Typically they may want to move the subject on quickly.*

  - *Wait out any embarrassed pauses, don't rush on, let the praise sink in*
  - *Repeat the praise later to give them a further chance to absorb it and accept it*

- ***It's not real***

  *Occasionally, people have experienced praise just as a way of buttering them up or making them pliable. It is then experienced as not real or manipulative.*

  - *Act out of Genuineness only*
  - *Be specific about what the particular praise is for*

- ***Minimising it as unimportant***

  *Occasionally someone might not see that a particular skill or action is important; they may take it for granted, overlooking it's significance. Positive reinforcement though will encourage people to do more of the same thing, and appreciate and value what they can contribute.*

  - *Reinforce the praise*
  - *Put it into context and explain why it is so important*

- ***Seeing it as a technique***

  *Basically, here the praise is not seen as being genuine, but artificial; something perhaps that has been introduced on the latest course.*

  - *Be genuine with the praise you give*
  - *Be consistent about giving it, but only when it is deserved*

# The Skills of Giving Negative Feedback

Negative Feedback is the other side of the equation which makes the whole. Although it is Positive Feedback which tends to reinforce High Performance the most, there will be occasions when Negative Feedback is necessary in the interests of the person, and to give a 'rounded' picture. Moreover, if people know that they will receive praise when due, this legitimises and makes acceptable the giving of Negative Feedback, and also makes the praise given to be experienced as valued and authentic.

### The Difference Between Technical Feedback and Reprimands

There are two types of Negative Feedback:



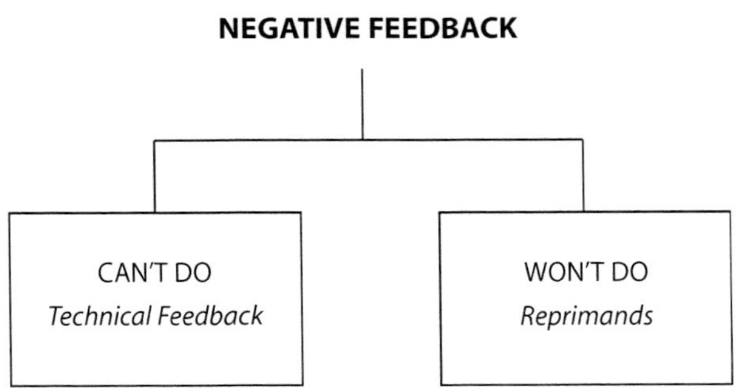


The first of these is where something has gone wrong, because of CAN'T DO, that is the team member didn't have the skills or knowledge to do what was required. The basic approach here is for the Leader to accept that this was his/her responsibility, and to deal with the situation neutrally as a piece of learning. Then again, people will sometimes make the wrong judgements or decisions, not out of any lack of WILL DO, but because their CAN DO is not yet fully developed. This also needs to be dealt with as a learning opportunity.

If the person has the skills and knowledge required, then it will be a WON'T DO situation, where a Reprimand is more appropriate. The way to deal with a Reprimand is:

- *Let people know, in advance, that you will be giving plenty of feedback*
- *Deal with poor performance immediately (but not in front of others)*
- *Stay in the I+U+ mode, remember it is not the person but his/her Behaviour that is at issue*
- *Describe explicitly the nature of the poor performance, its consequences and how you feel about it*
- *Pause for a second or two to allow the reprimand to sink in, look at the other person, let them feel your disappointment or displeasure*
- *Tell them what you require, and the consequences that will result*
- *Let them know you value them, but not their Behaviour on this occasion*
- *Move on to something else, the Reprimand is now over, it's done*

Again, it is useful to understand why people sometimes don't 'hear' Reprimands, and how to deal with Negative Reactions.

# Why People Sometimes Don't Hear Reprimands

- ***Shock***

  *"No-one has ever told me that before." Such news can confront someone's self image in a disturbing way.*

  - *Give time and space for the message to settle*
  - *Reinforce they are OK as a person (but not that particular Behaviour)*
  - *Remind them that you value them as a person, if not their Behaviour on this occasion*

- ***Denial***

  *"That's not right ... true ... accurate ... fair", or whatever. Here the person just plain refuses to consider the feedback as part of a defence mechanism.*

  - *Give specific behavioural examples to illustrate your point*
  - *Stay calm but persistent and assertive, refusing to be drawn into an argument*
  - *Seek agreement for them to think about what has been said*

- ***It's not fair***

  *The "It just came off in my hand, Mum" response, or "I'm better than many others, why pick on me?" approach. Here people are seeking to avoid responsibility for hearing the message by attempting to direct attention from themselves to elsewhere.*

  - *Refuse to discuss other people*
  - *Don't be diverted from the point, but be prepared to listen*

- ***Fear of being labelled/pigeonholed***

  *"This will be recorded somewhere", "I'll be seen this way for ever." The resistance is to do with the fear of being labelled as "blemished"*

  - *Take a future orientation*
  - *Remind them of their strengths, so the perspective is that of the whole picture*

- ***Anger at not being allowed to express their point of view***

  *"He's not listening to me so why should I bother listening to him? I'll switch off."*

  - *Listen*
  - *Demonstrate that you are listening by summarising, reflecting back, etc*
  - *If necessary, ask questions to draw the other person out*

# Dealing With Negative Reactions

| | |
|---|---|
| DISAGREEMENT | *Explain your view and listen actively to theirs; ask if they accept your view; agree to monitor the behaviour if necessary* |
| CHALLENGING | *Defuse aggression; lower your voice; stick to questions only for a time; say something positive about the person* |
| HURT SILENCE | *Allow emotional expression, ask "How do you FEEL about that?" Show that you care and that it is OK to be emotional. "That's OK, it's how you feel, tell me about it". Repeat strong praise and turn the conversation to the future* |
| TAKING MY BALL HOME | *Tackle the issue directly. "I can see you have taken that to heart", and ask questions to push the person into Challenging (see above)* |
| DEPENDENCY | *DON'T do all the work for them. Ask them, "What would you do to improve?" and don't be afraid of silences; wait for answers; push them into taking an active role* |

# Chapter Summary

- *Feedback allows people to know whether they are on course, or not, where they are, how they are doing.*
- *Feedback is also a powerful reward in its own sake, being an experience of recognition and praise which is relevant, real and central.*
- *'Catch People Doing Something Right'. Something right is an improvement, a step in the right direction, something different.*
- *Effective Feedback is given Assertively. Assertion is very different from Aggression, Submissiveness or Withdrawal.*
- *Being Assertive requires:*
  - *Staying in the I+U+ Position*
  - *Looking after your rights and the rights of the other person*
  - *Using '**I**' statements*
  - *Keeping what is said short and succinct*
  - *Avoiding 'Qualifiers'*
  - *Expressing your feelings*
  - *Avoiding irritators*
  - *Using appropriate body language*
- *Let people know, in advance, that you will be giving plenty of Feedback, both Positive and Negative, in order to help them improve.*
- *Address the Feedback to the Behaviour, not Personality or Values*
- *Be aware of the reasons why people sometimes don't hear praise or reprimands (negative feedback).*
- *There is a difference in Negative Feedback between Can't Do (Technical Feedback) and Won't Do (Reprimands).*

# chapter 8

# Motivation

## Different Strokes for Different Folks

- *The Importance of Motivation in the Performance Development Equation*
- *Understanding and Working with Individual Differences and Stages of Development*
- *Intrinsic and Extrinsic Motivation and Rewards*
  - *Key to Intrinsic and Extrinsic Motivators*
- *Lower and Higher Order Needs*
- *Situational Building Blocks for Motivation*
- *The Motivation Inventory – Understanding Yourself and Others*
  - *Motivation Inventory Categories*
  - *Interpretation and Review of Categories*
- *Motivation, Learning and Development*
- *'Dancing Dolphins'*
- *Level I and Level II Learning*
- *Transformational Development and Motivation*
- *Chapter Summary*

# The Importance of Motivation in the Performance Development Equation

| D2: Knows Individuals Needs and Motivations | *Relating to team members as individuals; realistic and knowledgeable about own and others' strengths and weaknesses; perceptive in knowing individuals' motivation patterns and needs, and skilled in providing appropriate rewards* |
| --- | --- |

Each one of us has things in common with other people but, at the same time, we are all uniquely different. Effective leaders are perceptive to and recognise such individual difference, respond well to it (while remaining situationally consistent) and treat their people as individuals, including providing appropriate Rewards and Consequences to help them develop. Being perceptive to individual difference matters greatly in helping someone to succeed and grow. This applies particularly with the levels and directions of motivation the individual has.



What is Motivation? It is the factors which cause, channel and sustain an individual's behaviour, leading to appropriate levels of commitment and effort in the situation (or not). Some of these factors are to do with the individual, some are to do with the situation s/he is in. A negative illustration of Motivation is the Won't Do (as opposed to the Can't Do) syndrome discussed in Chapter 5 – Diagnosing Performance Issues. In many ways Motivation is about 'will'.

All of us are likely to know people highly gifted in their natural abilities, and the skills and knowledge they possess, who have succeeded less well than someone else, with fewer natural abilities and less skill who, nevertheless, have put their abilities to better use. This highlights the importance of Motivation in performance. Additionally, when we think about particular situations we have experienced, we can readily see that the situation itself, and the way we saw it, had a major effect on our approach to it. As individuals we are likely to feel that we can (Skills) and want to (Motivation) cope much better with some situations than others, which can be represented like this:

**Performance = (Skills x Motivation) Situation**

# Understanding and Working with Individual Differences and Stages of Development

Getting knowledgeable about the other person, discovering and connecting with the needs they have, really matters in 'fine tuning' your approach in Developing High Performance, and more, in developing the person as a person. But it takes two to tango, and part of understanding the other person is in understanding yourself better. What follows should help in this also. The risk otherwise is seeing others just as an extension of yourself, with the same wants and needs, and perhaps on the basis that 'they should be just like me.' If this is the case then you won't make good contact.

*One real example of this is where a manager gave to a team member the exciting, challenging project of relocating a technical library and, at the same time, reorganising it to make it more efficient. Its present location was such that people could readily stop by for a chat, and the systems and procedures had grown in a topsy turvy way, without being thought through. The manager was highly enthusiastic about the opportunities involved when briefing the librarian.*

*However, nothing seemed to happen and the manager became increasingly irritated with the librarian's response, or lack of it. Finally, the penny dropped for the manager. He realised that he had been arrogant enough to assume that other people (and the librarian in particular) were like him, that is they wanted the same things and were stimulated and motivated to achieve them. When he thought about it more, he realised that part of his motivation pattern was achievement and challenge (hence his enthusiasm for the project), while the librarian's was more concerned with social needs (he actually enjoyed the interruptions) and security, preferring familiar ways of doing things.*

*The manager could see that he had presented what he thought was a marvellous opportunity to the librarian, but the librarian experienced it as a threat, not an opportunity. When he adjusted his approach to meet the motivational needs of the other person, and not just project his own, things started to happen and the project was completed well and on time.*



Huge sums of money have been spent on researching Motivation. There are no magic pills or formulas. What follows is a distillation of what is relevant to Developing High Performance, together with a powerful, practical tool for understanding patterns of Motivation.

# Intrinsic and Extrinsic Motivation and Rewards

Basically Motivation comes from within (Intrinsic) or without (Extrinsic). A fuller way of looking at this is that...

> ***INTRINSIC Rewards are 'psychological' ones experienced directly by the individual***
>
> ***EXTRINSIC Rewards are provided by an outside agent***

In its extreme form a cattle prod would be an example of Extrinsic Motivation, a less extreme example would be a bonus for completing a piece of work on time. An example of Intrinsic Motivation is where someone sets themselves a challenging task for the sense of achievement its completion brings about for them. Another example could be influencing someone to a point of view, or helping them achieve their goals.



> *Look again at the list of rewards shown in Chapter 6 – Rewards & Penalties. Which ones are Intrinsic and which are Extrinsic? The suggested answers are shown on page 154. The answers will not always be absolutely one way or the other. Sometimes the same reward can be perceived by one individual to be Extrinsic, while for another it will be Intrinsic. The new car parked on the driveway may represent achievement and self-esteem in an Intrinsic way, as well as material well-being. Equally, the cup of coffee a Leader hands to a team member can be symbolic as well as extrinsically material in that it can be a form of recognition which connects with what is inside the person, say the celebration of the satisfaction of a job well done.*
>
> *What is important in this is that Leaders who Develop High Performance:*
>
> - *Recognise the power of Intrinsic Motivation*
> - *Are highly alert to Individual Difference*

The problem with Extrinsic Motivation is that the stimulus has to be fuelled from outside, and is rarely self-sustaining. For example, one Sales Manager we worked with led his team almost entirely by the Extrinsic Motivation of attending sales conferences for achievement. Initially this worked very well, but it was not sustainable in the longer term and performance stabilised. Meanwhile another Sales Manager in the same company used Intrinsic as well as Extrinsic Rewards. He led his team in such a way that continued membership of the team became prized in itself, and each team member derived personal satisfaction from being party to the team's continued improvement. The performance of that branch came to far outstrip the other one. With many organisations too the Extrinsic Rewards are set out by the organisation and are not influenced greatly by an individual Leader. In such circumstances, once people are 'in' the organisation they can obtain many of these rewards by providing a 'tolerance' level of performance only.

A problem with Intrinsic Motivation on the other hand is that needs may be 'buried' in that it is not visible to the individual or the Leader. Habituation and situational factors, etc, all have an effect. The needs within a person may be dormant, suppressed or unrecognised until the right situation or stimuli are encouraged.

***SEEDS WHICH MAY HAVE LAIN DORMANT IN THE SOIL FOR DECADES CAN SPRING INTO LIFE WHEN SUNLIGHT CAN REACH THE AREA OF GROUND ONCE COVERED BY SHADE.***

Vincent Blood – Stewarts Nursery



***It is the Leader who creates the situation, the context, whether this be a productive and fulfilling one, a neutral one or a counter productive one.***

One example of changing needs (or needs which were perhaps there but not released, rather like a spring held in compression) occurred in a Civil Service Department, which had to adapt to a new, initiative-taking culture as part of a move from its traditional format into a Business Unit. This required staff to work in a more proactive and interdependent way than before. The energy released was analogous to the spring finding its natural form. Of course this wasn't true for everyone in the Unit, some found the move difficult because their source of motivation fitted with the old order of things, but a surprisingly large majority 'flowered' in the new situation.

It is Intrinsic Motivation that Leaders who Develop High Performance concentrate on most. Their access to substantial Extrinsic Rewards is usually limited anyway. This is not to say that such Extrinsic Rewards don't matter – the basic conditions/salary levels have to be perceived as reasonable otherwise they will act as a demotivator – but it is the Intrinsic ones which, generally speaking, are more powerful and sustainable in that the energy is released from within, not applied externally.

# Key to Intrinsic and Extrinsic Motivators

| | |
|---|---|
| **Money** | Generally **extrinsic**, but often with intrinsic connotations such as recognition, self worth and esteem. |
| **Promotion** | Generally **intrinsic**, but again often with some extrinsic considerations such as improved conditions/material rewards. |
| **Security** | Mostly **extrinsic**, but it can be **intrinsic** if the person feels they have a high degree of control over their future, eg being financially independent or having sought after prized skills. |
| **Recognition** | **Intrinsic.** Even when a material reward is given, eg a cup of coffee or a 'golden banana', this is more symbolic than extrinsic; that is, it is not the financial value which is important but what it means. |
| **Time Off** | Both **extrinsic** and **intrinsic** if given as a reward. |
| **Fun** | **Intrinsic.** |
| **Learning & Personal Growth** | Mostly **intrinsic**, especially where people wish to learn and grow, when it can be a very strong motivator. There can of course be an **extrinsic** component when it is seen, additionally, as a route to more material rewards. |
| **Interesting or Favourite Work** | **Intrinsic**, except when it is seen as avoiding, say, responsibility or difficult work. |
| **Ownership, Responsibility & Delegation** | **Intrinsic**. On an effort/material rewards basis it usually provides low, additional **extrinsic** rewards; nevertheless it is often a strong motivator. |
| **Job Satisfaction** | In terms of the definition, **intrinsic**. If it is to do with pay and contributions only, then it is **extrinsic**. |
| **Self Esteem & Worth** | **Intrinsic** |

*Sometimes the same reward can be experienced by the same people differently.*

# Lower and Higher Order Needs

There are many generalised theories or models of motivation. The problem with generalised approaches is that individual differences in strength of need are difficult to determine. Nevertheless they can give an overall perspective.

One of the best known of such approaches is Maslow's Hierarchy of Needs, and many of the other approaches are derived from this. Basically the Hierarchy of Needs says:

- *People have a number of needs, arranged as a hierarchy*
- *An individual is likely to be interested in fulfilling the next, higher, level of need in the hierarchy once their present one, and the need below it, have been largely satisfied*
- *The strength of a particular need will vary, individual to individual, but they all tend to apply to everyone in the order of importance shown*

**SELF-ACTUALISATION**
*Creative*
*Using full potential*
*Determiner of your own life*

**SELF-ESTEEM**
*Recognition*
*Feeling worthwhile*
*Respected*

**BELONGING**
*Love*
*Acceptance*
*Part of a Group*

**SECURITY**
*Protection from threat and danger*

**PHYSIOLOGICAL**
*Food*
*Water*
*Shelter*

Where do you feel you currently fit on this hierarchy and where are the members of your team? Are there any similarities ?

The 'higher order' needs will be seen to be Intrinsic ones, the 'lower order' ones Extrinsic. Note how Recognition and many of the 'Rewards' and 'Motivation' we have already talked about already fit in the hierarchy, and the importance of self-esteem.

Both the strength of a particular need and the way it is perceived and actioned will vary with individuals, which means just relying on the hierarchy is limited in its usefulness. Money, for example, may mean security for some, for others self-esteem (eg the big car in the drive), for others it can mean self-actualisation (such as building an enterprise, with the money giving some measure of the achievement). Some people may have low security and high self-actualisation needs, compared with others who have the reverse.



Usually Maslow is drawn as a pyramid; we have chosen to draw it as a tower of bricks, each one resting on the foundation of the one below it, so that if a lower one is removed those above it fall down. Change, or threatened change, often has this effect on people, so they become particularly concerned with their needs for security, and often (temporarily) less concerned with the higher order needs. In this situation people can sometimes be seen as behaving irrationally in their perception of the change, even though the change could benefit some of their higher order needs. Their immediate priority and concerns, however, will often be with security needs in this situation.

# Situational Building Blocks for Motivation

Before looking at a more comprehensive approach to understanding Motivation, it will be useful to remind ourselves of some basic rules and what has already been said about Developing High Performance - ie

**Performance = (Skills x Motivation) Situation**

*...it is the Leader who creates the context (the Situation)*

## Situational Factors

- ***Have High Expectations***

  *If your expectations about someone's performance are low or moderate, you will get just that. If your expectations are high (but not artificially or unrealistically so) you will tend to get that more. High Expectations are essential for the Challenge part of High Challenge-High Support.*

- ***Create Goal Focus and Clarity***

  *This is where Explicitness is important. There is a direct relationship between Goal Clarity and Motivation; if the Goal isn't clear and felt worthwhile, Motivation – even if high initially – won't be sustained. Such a situation can even be experienced as stressful.*

- ***Build (realistic) Self Esteem***

  *Enable and facilitate an early success and celebrate and build on it. Reinforce confidence. (Note, an extreme example of this is with disadvantaged children; it does not matter what the success is, the achievement of success means that the perception that success is not possible is changed to one where success in other areas becomes perceived as possible.)*

- ***Reinforce Good Performance***

  *'Catch someone doing something right' and encourage them to do more of the same, giving constant feedback.*

- ***Make the Performance Level Attainable***

  *If people feel the goal they are being asked to pursue is too difficult or impossible, or the effort/rewards balance is not right, their motivation will be low. This fits with working to a series of smaller steps, reinforced at each stage with rewards or consequences appropriate to the individual.*

- ***Work to 'Meta' Goals***

  *'Creating a world to which people want to belong' through Vision and Common Purpose, so their energies and Intrinsic Motivation is engaged. Developing, in partnership with them, the person as a person, say to personal mastery and creating their own success, and not just narrow task skills.*

- ***Provide High Support***

  *The necessary complement to High Challenge, but more than that, so that your relationship is valued and you are seen as an ally.*

- ***Apply Situational Leadership***

  *This is concerned with flexing your style to each person's level of development. It will be described in more detail in Chapter 9 – Situational Leadership & Consistency.*

# The Motivation Inventory – Understanding Yourself and Others

One way to start thinking about the individual members of your team is to simply think about what they do/like best.

> *Knowing the individual matters greatly*

A more comprehensive and complete way is through the Motivation Inventory which establishes, for an individual, their unique motivational patterns. The categories are shown on the following page. As you will see, although the factors are common (and provide a highly useful framework) it is the pattern and combination of the factors, and the relative weight placed on each one, that gives much insight. This brings us back to the notion that each one of us has things in common with other people but at the same time we are all uniquely different.



It is suggested that you use this framework to think about your own motivation patterns.

> *.... to understand others you first need to understand yourself ...*
>
> *and also as a way of helping to appreciate individual difference so you can better deal with people as individuals*

Be honest with yourself in identifying the six most important categories for you – then, of the six, the two most important of all. After that, identify which categories are least important for you. Don't have in mind what you think you should be, but rather who you are.

Then think about other members of your team, perhaps two people who are 'different' from each other – maybe even someone with whom you have a difficulty, and see if you can identify the important differences between them and you.

## Motivation Inventory Categories

| PEOPLE | |
|---|---|
| INFLUENCE | Persuading, communicating, developing; convincing people towards a course of action |
| SUPPORTING | Helping people achieve their goals; listening to them; providing close support as well as time and attention |
| GREGARIOUSNESS | Meeting and working with a wide range of people, including the public |
| SOLITUDE | Having space to get on with things without contact or distraction from other people |
| AFFILIATION | Having close relationships; being part of a team; working interdependently with others and being liked and respected by them |
| DEDICATION | Helping the company's wider society and the community; doing something worthwhile; making the world a better place to be |
| RELATING | Responding to different individual needs; dealing with difficult interpersonal situations; trusting and being trusted; resolving conflict |
| **ACHIEVEMENT** | |
| TASK FOCUS | Having a liking for detail and analysis; using skills and knowledge; enjoying specific tasks, intellectual challenge; focusing on the job in hand |
| GOAL ORIENTATION | Working to targets; a future perspective to achieve tangible results; output rather than input focused; problem solving; satisfying customers and providing good service; achieving business results |
| POWER & AUTHORITY | Having control over others; being able to direct them and control work and events; making big decisions; being regarded as the source of authority |
| RESPONSIBILITY | Leading others; taking and accepting responsibility for decisions; making a difference; doing what is necessary to ensure company success; representing others |

| | |
|---|---|
| INITIATIVE & INTERDEPENDENCE | Using own initiative; dislike of bureaucracy and red tape; operating independently; deciding own course of action |
| CREATIVITY | Generating ideas; producing something new; finding new ways |
| CHALLENGE | Being stretched; liking energy and hard work and competitive situations; responding to pressure and deadlines; being active and challenged |
| **ENJOYMENT** | |
| SUITABILITY | Comfort in knowing capability to do job based on previous experience; perceived match of knowledge and skills |
| STRUCTURE | Operating to guidelines and systems; organising and planning; meeting standards; creating order, procedure and systems |
| SECURITY | Job security; knowing what is going on; a liking for certainty |
| TANGIBLE REWARD | Money; status; glamour; perks |
| VARIETY & FUN | Enjoyment and fun; difference; travel; location; not repetitive or being bored |
| RECOGNITION | Being well regarded and appreciated; feeling good about self and work; self development |
| COMFORT | Working moderate hours; not dealing with unpleasant or difficult situations; keeping clear of anxiety and stress; avoiding failure |



## Interpretation and Review of Categories

The first thing to do is to compare the overall balance between People, Achievement and Enjoyment. Effective Leaders and Developers of High Performance tend to have both high Achievement and People motivation (High Challenge for *achievement* – High Support). Sufficient Enjoyment is required to enable people not to become overly stressed or to develop tunnel vision.

Now start to explore the various factors within each general category. For example, it will soon be seen that the expression that 's/he is a people person' is meaningless; the person may have a strong orientation towards others, but is it to influence them or be liked, to dominate or support, to just be with people or to have deeper relationships with them? In the world of work, having high People motivation is usually not enough by itself, it needs to be coupled with Achievement to secure movement, otherwise it just becomes a social or friendship group with no task focus.

This can be illustrated by looking at the profile for a successful Leader, who will be goal rather than task focused, has reasonably high responsibility needs (but not high power and authority ones), welcomes being able to use initiative and actively wants challenge. They will want to influence people, be comfortable with working with a range of them, will have a team orientation without being submerged by the team, and will want to support team members, but not to the degree that they lose sight of the achievement part of the equation.

There are other factors too. For example, the technical expert is likely to relish challenge, applied with a task focus where a prized skill can be used (*Suitability*) within a structure. Another example would be the combination of high structure and low independence needs, which tend to result in difficulty with being flexible and solving problems, or people with high challenge and low suitability who sometimes bite off more than they can chew. Equally, people who do not want to be distracted by others (*Solitude*) concentrating on the mixture of tasks without much need for variety, can be worth their weight in gold in one context, and fearfully inappropriate in another.

This is where it is well worth understanding the different sources of People, Achievement and Enjoyment motivation. There is all the difference in the world, for example, between task focus and goal orientation; both are important forms of Achievement motivation, but they differ in kind.

Potential problems can occur when there is perhaps too little or too much of a particular type of motivation. For example, being overly high on independence and initiative can mean that the person is difficult to manage; being very low can result in dependence. The opposite side of this coin is that ignoring a team member's need for support can result in high stress; too much support can smother. Remember too that there are no 'perfect' people – rather there are relative strengths and weaknesses for a particular job.

What will have been noticed is that many of these motivation factors, and the rewards that come with them, are intrinsic ones. They come from within the person, they are part and parcel of him or her, and the satisfaction of the need brings the reward – eg challenge. They are more to do with what people put into the job – possibly, of course, their manager encourages, facilitates and recognises this, largely through knowing the motivation pattern of the person. Other rewards are extrinsic, the stimulus is provided to the person, such as with tangible rewards and variety, and are more to do with what people 'get out' of the job.

In this connection, if the motivation pattern is one of low People and Achievement motivation, and extremely high Enjoyment requirements – such as high pay, much glamour and status, fun, variety and travel – with little challenge and hard work, the expectation may be a little unrealistic, particularly in today's world (*"I've been trying to find a job like that for years"*). It is sometimes a characteristic of people who are strongly dissatisfied with their jobs, or series of jobs.



One of the advantages of frameworks such as the Motivation Inventory is that they enable you to think more clearly about not only yourself, but the people you work with. Within your group there will be similarity as well as much difference; being perceptive about the differences will help in adjusting your approach, style and even rewards, to different people. It is a case of different strokes for different folks, while monitoring your situational consistency.

It is important, too, not to let your own profile, or prejudices even, blind you to the difference in others. Because you are one person, with a particular set of primary sources of motivation, it does not mean that those who differ from you are wrong, but just different, often with the richness that this can bring. Above all, to understand others, the first person who must be understood is yourself.

# Motivation, Learning and Development

The way we approach situations such as change and learning is strongly influenced by the mindset or Underlying Beliefs we have. We have stressed that the particular 'lens' through which Leader/ Developers see their world is crucial to their effectiveness as Leader/Developers, **and** that the truly successful ones operate to the principle of both High Challenge and High Support. In this sense it is the Leader who defines the situation and, if s/he is successful, helps the team members to redefine it for themselves. Such redefinitions, or shift of mindset, is the crucial part of real, continual and sustained learning and development.



The mind set of the Command and Control system of managing (which many of us have been subject to, or have applied) was useful perhaps in many previous situations, but only up to a point. For it is not the way to cause the 'meta' vision of people performing at their very best to happen, and it is certainly not the way to enable people to use their initiative responsibly and well. It is sometimes said that the Transactional skills used in the Developing Stage of the Developing High Performance process, are those of the classic reinforcement approach – stimulus response, reinforcement - and concentrate on behaviour change only, and that is to some extent true. But such a Transactional approach is often necessary to realise a satisfactory level of performance. Then there are situations where it is important to prescribe and reinforce the right way - safety and some operating procedures being a case in point. It is, or should be, part of a stage in the journey of development, the other stages being the ones of Developing and Enabling, that is the Transformational part of the whole High Challenge-High Support approach.

> *This involves creating a world in which people want to belong, to which they relate with commitment and not just compliance, and where the driving force comes from their own internal motivation.*

# Dancing Dolphins'

Rather than visioning people like pigeons, or computers even, porpoises and dolphins provide much more respectful and appropriate insights for understanding human behaviour. Again, this is not to say that people are dolphins, it is simply that because dolphins are studied in ways which people are not, the results provide a useful way of understanding certain forms of learning. Next to humans, porpoises and dolphins are regarded as the most intelligent beings; more their creativity and ability to use discretion and judgement is large.

It is the exercise of Creativity and Discretion – doing what is right at the time – which Transformational Leaders seek to develop in their people, to equip them for the rigours of today's world. This is achieved through the Developing and Enabling Stages of the process, and leads to Independence and Interdependence.



*Research involving the training of dolphins has shown that:*

- *They are extremely sensitive to the **context** of their training.*

  *The context includes the reasons for the training, why they are doing it and for whom, other participants, the location etc*

- *They are extremely sensitive to their **relationship** with the trainer (Leader/Developer)*

In order to effectively train a dolphin you must establish a relationship with it, otherwise it will ignore you - even if you are the one who feeds it. In a people/organisational setting, 'feeding' is represented by pay, and the relationship has to be more than just being the hierarchical leader; a relationship built on Personal Power, Positive Regard, Genuineness and Trust will be necessary. Also necessary will be some identification with the reasons and purpose of the training – ie that it is legitimate.

Some other relevant findings were:

- *Occasionally the dolphin became increasingly disturbed and frustrated at being 'wrong' and the trainer found it necessary to give the dolphin an unearned fish to preserve the relationship, for if the dolphin became too frustrated with the trainer it would refuse to co-operate.*

  *Here we can extrapolate the need for continued support and encouragement, not punishment, in times of difficulty and when the situation is high Will Do, low Can Do, and also the importance of maintaining the effort/reward balance through achievable steps.*

- *Sometimes dolphins would go wild with excitement, putting on an elaborate performance including displaying many completely original behaviours, having made a 'break through'. It had put things together for itself (in non-dolphin dialect 'the penny had dropped') and there was a thrill in the learning that needed to be caught and celebrated.*

  *In the organisation setting it matters greatly that the Leader/Developer is a partner in catching and celebrating that 'break through'. This 'break through' was connected with the third and crucially important point below, it had learned* ***classes*** *of behaviour, not just behaviour.*

- *Classes of behaviour are different from a particular behaviour in that the connections, or learning, came from the dolphin (or person) themselves. It is learning to learn, not just responding to a particular stimulus or reward, where the learning of new tasks gets faster and faster, particularly when they fall into the same class of activity, enabling 'learning leaps' to be made.*

# Level I and Level II Learning

We can see that there are at least two types of learning, which we will call Level I and Level II.

| | |
|---|---|
| LEVEL I | Based on stimulus, response, reinforcement, so that behaviour is changed through the Transactional actions of the Leader/Developer such as the Developing stage of the Leading and Developing High Performance Process. |
| LEVEL II | Learning to recognise the larger context in which the stimulus is occurring so its **meaning** can be correctly interpreted. This requires a will, or motivation to learn, such motivation coming from the person themselves. |



Learning leaps are to do with learning changes of behaviour. Clearly the ability to learn patterns this way involves more than simple stimulus/response/reinforcement sequences for isolated behaviours, and involves Attitudes as well as Skills and Behaviours. It is the Developing and Enabling Stages of the Leading and Developing High Performance Process.

Although Level II does involve reinforcement, it is of a different type than simple reinforcement for task learning. The reinforcement is for 'exploration', that is, in using Responsible Initiative in trying new things out.

# Transformational Development and Motivation

The ability to explore, to learn to exercise Responsible Initiative, judgement or to be creative is a higher level of learning than the specific behaviours which make up these abilities, not least because they involve Attitudes or Mindsets, and not just Behaviours. The processes and dynamics at this level are Transformational, for the Stages in the process are the Developing and Enabling ones, and they require a quality of relationship between the Leader/Developer and the team

| | |
|---|---|
| Developing and Enabling involves: | ▪ *Creating a world to which people want to belong:*<br>– *which they relate to with commitment and not just compliance*<br>– *where the driving force is their own internal motivation, released* |
| Leader/Developers who are effective in the Developing and Enabling Stages of the Process: | ▪ *Use Transformational Skills as well as Transactional ones*<br>▪ *Establish productive, trusted relationships with their people*<br>▪ *Encourage Level II learning opportunities*<br>▪ *Work at the level of Mindset or Attitudes as well as Behaviour*<br>▪ *Continue to provide Supportive Feedback which reinforces the internal motivation of the individuals*<br>▪ *Provide a context in which it is safe to learn*<br>▪ *Maintain High Challenge as well as High Support* |
| Their aim is to help equip their people to: | ▪ *Operate Interdependently using Responsible Initiative*<br>▪ *Take responsibility for their own continuous learning and development* |

Here the role of Leader/Developer is to create and manage the context and relationship in which people can excel instead of simply telling them what to do. The thrust becomes not to 'condition' specific behaviours, but rather to get the person to be creative within their own natural set of behaviours. The success of the Leader/Developer is based on his/her ability to 'draw out' or release the potential abilities of the person. This involves encouraging the person to learn to generate new behaviours on their own, within the boundaries and context of the task to be performed. The Leader/Developer here is not some uninvolved distant observer, but rather is part of the situation, relating to the person and genuinely wanting them to succeed, and having set the High Challenge maintains a relationship of High Support.

Feedback is still important, but the context and underlying message of this feedback is

> *You are in a situation in which it is safe to learn and to challenge yourself. The amount that you can learn and grow depends on your own initiative. It's okay to try new things and make mistakes. Nothing bad will happen to you if your mistakes are genuine ones. What is most important is that you do your personal best, and continually develop your ability, flexibility and professional mastery so that you become 'the best you can be'. You will be assisted and helped by supportive feedback.*



What is Supportive Feedback in this situation? It is **information** to the person, based on observation about particular behaviours, coupled with **motivation and meaning** – that is, what was liked about the behaviour – to encourage the person to do more of it and to continually search for ways to improve.

Feedback provides motivation when the information is made more meaningful through the individual being able to connect it with what they have done and make sense of it. Here the power of the motivation is not the outside stimulus, or a material reward, the motivation is internal, the reinforcement being that the feedback gives meaning to what has been done and the reward comes from the individual themselves.

There is another type of feedback too which is important at this stage. This is the 'unearned fish' or positive comments, such as the unconditional praise or encouragement which supports and maintains the all important relationship between the two people. All this of course is part of continuing support.

However, High Support, by itself, can create an illusion of success only because everything can be seen as positive. This is where it is so important to keep the *High Challenge-High Support* balance right, but, and it is an important **BUT**, one also where the team member increasingly participates in creating challenging situations for themselves that lead to this growth. This is part and parcel of people taking responsibility for their own learning and development, continuous improvement and becoming self-directing.

This is what Level II learning is all about. It is to do with becoming enabled, to do what is required using Responsible Initiative in the fast moving situations of today, where flexibility, coping with new and perhaps unfamiliar situations is so important. Of course, if a particular procedure needs to be followed, perhaps for safety or operational reasons, then a Level I approach focused on the explicit behavioural level of what the person is required to do, may be appropriate. But usually, having the 'end in mind' at the start of the whole process, the Vision of seeing people becoming '*the best they can be*', required people taking on the habits and approach of being Interdependent, not Dependent or Counter Dependent - in short, using Responsible Initiative.



For this to be caused to happen, or allowed to happen in some cases, Level II learning has to be encouraged and sustained, which involves self-motivated activity on the part of the learner. This is the key, the Transformational trigger, that the really effective Leader/Developers work towards, action and achieve.

# Chapter Summary

- *Each one of us has things in common with other people but, at the same time, we are all uniquely different. Being perceptive to individual differences matters greatly in helping someone to succeed and develop.*
- *Motivation is what leads to effort in a situation, or not. In many ways, it is about will, it is the Will Do, or Won't or Don't Want To Do, factor.*
- *In performance issues and development, it is usually Motivation which matters most, often more so than Skills.*
- ***Performance = (Skills x Motivation) Situation***
- *Different people have differing types and levels of Motivation; real connection with a person is only made when their Motivation pattern is understood.*
- *There are no magic pills or potions, but there are ways to see what matters to the person, and to respond to that.*
- *Motivation comes from within (Intrinsic) or from without (Extrinsic) a person. Intrinsic Motivation is more self-sustaining.*
- *It is Intrinsic Motivation which effective Leader/Developers concentrate on. The basic Extrinsic Rewards have to be reasonable, firstly however.*
- *Effective Leader/Developers start with getting the basics right. These include:*
  - *Having high expectations*
  - *Creating goal focus and clarity*
  - *Building (realistic) self-esteem*
  - *Reinforcing good performance*
  - *Making the performance level attainable*
  - *Working to 'Meta' goals*
  - *Providing high support*
  - *Flexing style to levels of development*

chapter 9

# Situational Leadership and Consistency Adapting Your Leadership Style Appropriately

- *Factors which Influence Effective Situational Leadership*
- *Style Effectiveness, Style Flexibility and Situational Consistency*
- *The Directing, Coaching, Mentoring & Enabling Styles*
- *Leadership Style & Rewards*
- *Putting Leadership Styles to Work*
- *The Situation as the Leader Defines It*
  - *Transactional and Transformational Situational Leadership*
- *Style Characteristics, When to Use and Tips in Applying*
- *Assessing Development Levels for Particular Tasks*
  - *Assessing Levels of Development Maturity*
- *Chapter Summary*

# Factors which Influence Effective Situational Leadership

| D1: Flexes Style Appropriately: | *Deals with individuals on the basis of what they do, not what they are; everyone knows clearly where they stand and that particular behaviours are responded to in consistent, particular ways; is able to flex style appropriately to deal with various levels of performance and commitment to overall vision* |
|---|---|



Situational Leadership and Consistency is concerned with the adjustment of style and approach by the Leader in response to a particular situation. Used well and proactively, it also causes and creates new situations such as accelerated development or improved performance. Equally, if the style used is inappropriate, rigid or inconsistent, then it will have a negative impact on the team member's performance.

**No one style is effective in all situations**. If, for example, there is a sudden fire in the workplace then very clear direct Leadership (to the next exit) is likely to be effective; where to go for a drink after work will be open to the views of everyone involved.

Some of the factors which influence the situation are:

- ***The Leader's Past Experience and Expectations***

  *If the Leader has used a particular style in the past and it has worked well, then the tendency is for that Leader to stick to that style, even though the situation changes, instead of responding flexibly to the new situation. Also a self-fulfilling prophecy applies in that if the Leader expects low (or high) performance, the expectations will influence the results.*

- ***The Leader's Expectations and Behaviour***

  *People tend to model themselves on their own Leader, and such Leaders have much influence on people reporting to them. Change programmes often fail because although senior managers espouse new behaviours, they sometimes fail to carry them out themselves.*

- ***Peers' Expectations and Behaviour***

  *For example, whether they operate to competition or co-operation.*

- ***Organisational Culture and Policies***

  *"The way things are done around here." The general direction is a move from a Command and Control culture to a more Enabling one. This sometimes creates difficulties for Leaders who lack the flexibility to adjust their styles, or are actually more at home with Command and Control.*

- ***Task Requirements***

  *Jobs that require precise instructions and the following of exact procedures (eg quality inspection) require a Leadership style that will differ say, from that required for jobs where the way they are carried out can vary, or where discretion can be used (eg customer service).*

- ***Team Members' Characteristics, Expectations and Behaviour***

  *The Skills and Attitudes of team members also influence the Leader's choice of style. The starting position may be that highly capable members require a less directive approach. Also while some people want to be directed, others prefer taking responsibility for their own work. Whatever the starting position, it is not necessarily fixed for all time, the situation is open to influence by the Leader – as will now be discussed.*

# Style Effectiveness, Style Flexibility and Situational Consistency

The appropriateness of style used depends more than anything else on the ability of the Leader to:

- *select the right style for the situation (STYLE EFFECTIVENESS)*

  *and*

- *use an appropriate range of styles matched to the situation (STYLE FLEXIBILITY)*

***This will result in SITUATIONAL CONSISTENCY***



To do this well requires an understanding of the individual, as an individual, and what might be called their 'maturity' in terms of the way they go about and approach their job role. In looking at 'maturity', where they are on the Dependency through to Interdependency voyage also matters greatly.

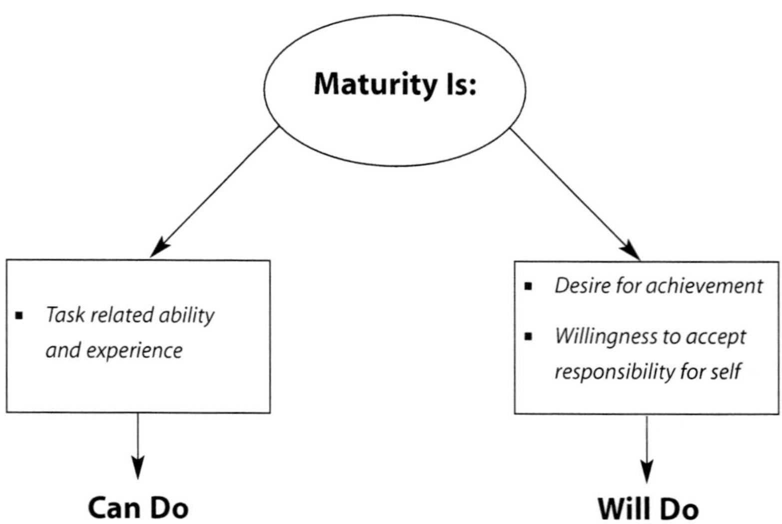

The Can Do/Can't Do and Will Do/Won't Do syndrome was described previously in Chapter 5 - Diagnosing Performance Issues.

One way of looking at Situational Leadership is through the following model:

**LEADERSHIP STYLES & SITUATIONAL CONSISTENCY SUMMARY**

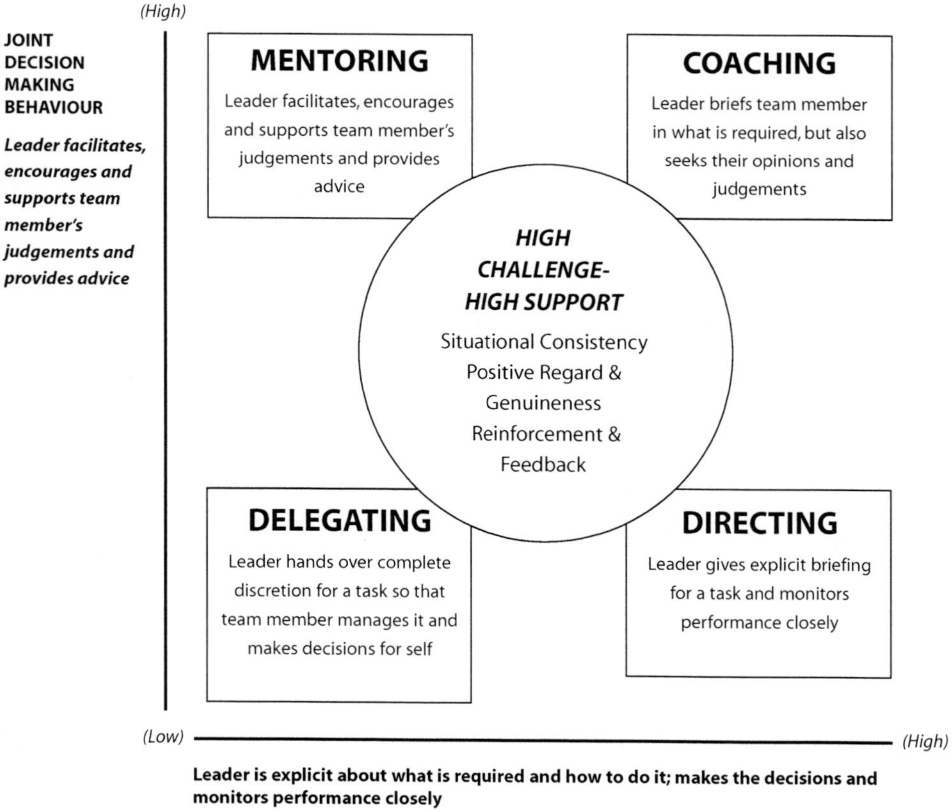


*Based on Blanchard, Zigarmi & Zigarmi 1985*

# The Directing, Coaching, Mentoring and Delegating Styles

Here there are four basic styles, or phases – phases in the sense that as team members develop and 'mature' the Leader adapts his/her style to meet the new 'situation'.
The first style is Directing, where the Leader gives explicit briefing for a task and monitors performance closely. The skills of Explicitness and Assertion come very much into play here and, in fact, Directing is the style most appropriate to the Mobilising stage of the whole approach (Chapter 3).

- ***Directing***

  *Directing, as a style, can be appropriate, initially for someone new to the team or organisation, where that person is unfamiliar with the organisation and the way things are done, or unfamiliar with the task. A non-Directive style here might cause anxiety and confusion, as it also might where major change is being carried out. The 'Directness' in these situations can provide the comfort of 'knowing where you are' which was illustrated earlier by the 'skating in the dark on top of a skyscraper analogy' described earlier.*

  *Of course 'Directness' does not imply lack of Positive Regard, or discourtesy. There is, however, a trap to look out for. This is causing the team member to become dependent on you to always tell him/her what to do, particularly with people who are inclined or habituated towards Dependency anyway. Overuse of this style, without moving to others, can encourage such Dependency.*

  *One other situation where the Directing style can be highly appropriate is in the performance issue of Can't Do, or Won't do, or perhaps a combination of both. Facing, dealing with and resolving such issues usually requires Directness, not through 'bawling out' or admonition, but in the ways previously described.*

- ***Coaching***

  *The next style, in sequence, is the Coaching one, where the Leader briefs the team member on what is required, but also seeks their opinions and judgements. Although the Leader is still providing guidance, s/he also provides explanations and opportunities for clarification and suggestions. Both the Leader and the team member are involved in deciding how to approach the task, although it is the Leader, with this style, who finally decides the course of action.*

*Coaching is used increasingly when the Leader becomes satisfied that the person largely has the capability to do what is required and some willingness to do so. This style is used to encourage further efforts on the part of the team member, and to demonstrate trust and support, even though they may not be ready or able yet to accept full responsibility for the task. Because it is 'involving', Coaching is also a good learning style as it promotes active learning (instead of the passive learning of the Directing style) through a structure of guidance, with the safety net of the Leader still keeping a close eye on results. When the situation moves to a first flowering of Can Do and Will Do it is the style to use, so it fits, as does Mentoring in a more advanced way, with the Developing stage of the whole approach.*

- ***Mentoring***

  *In the third phase, the Mentoring one, the team member's ability and motivation to take responsibility has increased, or is such already that the Leader facilitates, encourages and supports the team member's judgement and provides advice, rather than the more directive guidance of the Directing and Coaching Styles. Indeed close Direction is likely to be resented.*

  *However, the Leader will still need to provide High Support, recognition and encouragement if the fourth stage is to be achieved. For, at the Mentoring stage, although the Can Do may be high, there still may be wrinkles to learn to achieve professional mastery, and the Will Do may need to be underpinned by greater self-confidence.*

- ***Delegating or Enabling***

  *The fourth stage is Enabled Delegation; enabled because it rarely happens by itself. Here the Leader hands over complete discretion for a task, so that the team member manages it and makes the decisions for him/herself, because they are now self-directing, experienced and confident. They are on their own, flying solo –* ***but they are not alone*** *– you, the Leader, are there providing not interference but backup, encouragement, recognition and continuous support, dealing with mistakes as learning opportunities rather than as a chance to demonstrate that you knew best all along.*

It is your style which alters, not the underlying framework of *High Challenge-High Support* you operate to with its high expectations, Positive Regard, regular feedback and reinforcement. You have delivered this throughout and will continue to do so even when the person is able and willing to operate to Enabled Delegation. The Leader's task is now to sustain the team member there, not just to manage 'by exception' -that is, only giving feedback (negative) when a mistake is made and giving no recognition apart from that.

Applying the appropriate style according to how individuals behave in terms of their Can Do and Will Do capability and preparedness is Situational Consistency – or giving the same kinds of 'strokes to different folks' for the same kind of behaviour and doing so consistently and thoroughly. This also applies with the range of tasks an individual is required to perform; in one task someone may be at the Mentoring stage, at another, which is completely unfamiliar to them, the Directing style would be more appropriate. If the Leader is Situationally Consistent then the team member will know how the Leader operates (the 'rules of engagement', so to speak), and the use of different styles for different tasks where the level of competence varies, will not present problems – rather it will be experienced as helpful and facilitating.

# Leadership Style and Rewards

Clearly there is a strong connection between Leadership Style and Rewards. Being trusted, being given responsibility, using one's own judgement, receiving praise, developing skills are examples of Rewards and Recognition for many people (but not all). Equally, the same Rewards can be experienced as a threat, or even punishment, by others - such as might be the case in someone lacking in self-confidence who you want to encourage to take more responsibility and be more self-directing. Or perhaps one of your team members is struggling to cope with change and is stuck at a particular stage in the transition curve.
In such cases, the steps taken may need to be more gradual and reinforced with greater support. Generally speaking, though, people tend to welcome increased control of what they do at work.

On occasions, it will be legitimate to revert back to an earlier style. Sometimes this will happen when you have mistakenly over-estimated someone's 'maturity', such as when their Can Do is not as well developed as you originally thought. Reverting to the previous style will rectify the situation and can be more helpful, for the time being, to the team member. (Make sure that you don't get stuck with or encourage Dependency however).

Flexing your Leadership Style can also be used to give Penalties or Consequences as well as Rewards. If someone has been trusted with responsibility, say, through an Enabling or Mentoring style, and that trust is used irresponsibly, then the 'punishment' could be to take away much of that responsibility, for the time being, by reverting to a Coaching or Directing style. Or if someone has, perhaps after much effort, started to carry out a new task to your satisfaction so that you start to use a Coaching instead of a Directing style, and for a while they are fine but then their standards start to slip, you may need to get them back on course by some Directing. When the issue is a Won't Do and not a Can't Do, then it is a reprimand situation, and the penalty may include being supervised more closely.

# Putting Leadership Styles to Work

We suggested earlier that a useful way of looking at Performance was through seeing it as the result of (Skills x Motivation) Situation. Another way of looking at it, is to say ...

**Performance = (Can Do x Will Do) Situation**

In this, the Situational Factors matter greatly and include those factors, described earlier, which relate to the job such as task requirements, organisational culture and policies, etc. The match between the level of skills required for the job in its entirety, and the degree of discretion built into it, is all-important. For example, a nurse in an operating theatre will be required to carry out set procedures, while a customer services representative may be required to use much more individual discretion and initiative in handling certain situations.



How team members perceive and define a Situation, will depend on their expectations, past experiences, attitudes and characteristics. For example, one person may see an opportunity while another sees the same situation as a threat. In a situation of change one team member may be stuck in a passive resistance mode while another is adapting well to that new situation. As part of the perception of the situation, too, the Effort-Reward bargain will be taken into account - that is, individuals come to a view as to whether they want the reward (or avoidance of consequences) sufficiently to put in the effort required.

# The Situation as the Leader Defines It

Leadership Style is very much to do with how the Leader defines the situation, and his/her past experience and expectations, and perhaps the expectations of his/her manager, can have a major influence. For example, a Leader may not believe in Enabling, preferring to be strongly Directing, or may not look at Style Flexibility and Skill to adjust style appropriately. The Leader then becomes locked into a narrow range of styles which in turn influences the way the situation is perceived by him/her.

A common style profile, in the UK at least, is often a diluted Coaching one, backed up by Mentoring, even when the situation plainly calls for a Directing or Enabling approach, or even the ability to switch appropriately, with Situational Consistency, between all four.



> *The situation is not passive or fixed; it is the Leader*
>
> *who can change the situation - the job related Situational Factors,*
>
> *the situation as the Leader defines it.*
>
> *EFFECTIVE LEADERS **CREATE** THE SITUATION FOR THE TEAM'S SUCCESS*

There are a number of levels to this, which relate to Leadership Style and Situational Consistency. The first results in a low or poor level of effectiveness, where the style used is rigid or inappropriate, where nothing is ever changed, or attention and feedback (negative) are only given when things go wrong. (The behaviour here is mistakenly believed to amount to Delegation).

The other two levels, more positively, give rise to effective performance, with the second of these being more far reaching and powerful than the first in Developing High Performance. Both depend on the Leader defining the situation, in particular ways, so that s/he acts as either a Transactional or a Transformational Leader, described first in Chapter 3 – What High Performance Leaders Actually Do.

- ***Transactional Situational Leadership***

  *This is the fundamental level. Transactional Situational Leaders identify what team members need to do to achieve the organisational goals, consider the situation, and help their people to be competent and confident in achieving such goals. The Leader will judge what kind of style is appropriate for a particular situation, taking into account the 'maturity' of the skill and motivation of team members, their individual needs and their dignity. As part of this latter they will flex their approach to synchronise well with the individual. For example, someone who is knowledgeable and long-serving might expect to be treated more like a peer than a subordinate.*

  *Such Transactional Leadership, when it is carried out well, will be flexible and at the same time Situationally Consistent. It requires perception and the recognition that no one style is suitable for all situations, and the Leader who wants to develop people so that they learn their work and increase their confidence and competence will have to adapt their style consistently.*

  *All this matters at the most fundamental level of Leadership; it is straightforward, everyday and, essentially, action based. There is another way of looking at Leadership, however, in which the Leader defines the situation in a wider and more powerful way.*

- ***Transformational Situational Leadership***

  *Transformational Leadership 'motivates us to do more than we originally expected to do' by raising the sense of the importance and value of our tasks, by connecting us to the interests of the team and organisational purpose, and by raising the consciousness of our higher order, Intrinsic needs. It differs in degree from Transactional Situational Leadership in that it employs a higher degree of Vision. Vision has to do with creating images of future goals, while action has to do with immediate behaviours.*

# Style Characteristics, When to Use and Tips in Applying

| **1. DIRECTING** | |
|---|---|
| **Characteristics of Directing** | *Here the Leader is very explicit about what is to be done and how it is to be done, and works very closely with a team member who is inexperienced about the particular task, or does not have the 'will' to carry it out well. The team member is allowed little discretion.*<br>▪ *The Leader knows precisely how the work is best carried out*<br>▪ *Very detailed instructions are given by the Leader*<br>▪ *There is little or no room for the team member to use discretion*<br>▪ *The work is closely monitored, with each stage checked and corrected before the next stage*<br>▪ *All decisions are made by the Leader* |
| **When to use the Directing Style** | ▪ *The team member has a low level of competence in the task or a low level of 'will do'*<br>▪ *When mistakes, such as with safety, quality etc, cannot be left to chance*<br>▪ *To get team members off to a fast start with new tasks*<br>▪ *When the right habits need to be formed from the beginning* |
| **Tips in Applying the Directing Style** | ▪ *Explain why you are using this style and how you are subsequently likely to use other styles which allow more involvement*<br>▪ *Maintain Positive Regard and the team member's self esteem; you are using this style to help him/her in the particular situation*<br>▪ *Be explicit, clear and direct, breaking up the 'Direction' into manageable chunks*<br>▪ *Give reasons/explanations why you want things carried out in a certain way*<br>▪ *Reinforce good performance – 'catch people doing something right' - and be ready to move to the next stage* |

| 2. COACHING | |
|---|---|
| **Characteristics of Coaching** | *Here the team member has a good basic understanding of what is required, and importantly wants to do it well or perhaps with more confidence, and is ready to take on more responsibility for simple decisions involved in the task. The Leader involves the team member more in how the task is to be done, moving away from just telling and explaining, to seeking opinions or getting the team member to start to exercise judgement. At the same time, the Leader retains sufficient control to prevent significant mistakes and to keep overall direction.*<br>▪ *The Leader does not closely supervise the basic task but requires to be kept fully involved in the decision making process*<br>▪ *The Leader encourages the team member to make suggestions about how to proceed or how to deal with particular problems*<br>▪ *If there is disagreement on what should be done the Leader makes the final decision* |
| **When to use the Coaching Style** | ▪ *The team member has sufficient basic competence to be trusted to carry out the task and sufficient motivation (Will Do) to want to do it well*<br>▪ *Judgement, discretion and Responsible Initiative are being used by the team member, but still need further development*<br>▪ *The Leader still has much more competence in the particular task than the team member and the transfer of that competence to the team member is some way from being complete*<br>▪ *The team member lacks the confidence, yet, to 'fly solo', or perhaps is over-confident so that discretion is used irresponsibly.* |

| | |
|---|---|
| **Tips in Applying the Coaching Style** | ▪ *Do not allow people to become dependent on you (flattering though that may be), always push for suggestions from the team member about how to deal with issues*<br>▪ *Ask for their opinions, give yours and explain any decisions when you override them*<br>▪ *Be consistent in requiring to be kept informed; when people have demonstrated that they can be trusted to do what is required, tell them so*<br>▪ *Don't revert to the Directing Style at the first 'Can't Do' mistake*<br>▪ *Provide lots of encouragement and support, use the Coaching Style clearly and strongly where the situation fits, and not as a 'cop out' for Directing* |



| **3. MENTORING** | |
|---|---|
| **Characteristics of Mentoring** | *This is the style to use when the team member has a good competence in the particular task, reasonable experience in it, and has consistently demonstrated high 'Will Do.' The team member can be trusted to deal with most issues without the intervention of the Leader, but may still need, and feel the need for, direct support when difficult or unusual decisions are to be made, or where an unusual feature occurs which hasn't been experienced before by the team member.*<br>▪ *The Leader acts as a supportive 'colleague' in drawing out the team member's own ideas, helping by talking them through; being a sounding board*<br>▪ *The Leader makes observations or raises issues which need to be dealt with, but works to encourage team members to produce solutions*<br>▪ *Decisions on routine matters are always made by the team member, decisions in new or difficult areas are made by joint problem solving*<br>▪ *The Leader positions team members to make good decisions by briefing them regularly on wider organisational issues* |

| | |
|---|---|
| **When to use the Mentoring Style** | ▪ *The team member has good competence in the particular tasks, together with demonstrated judgement and high 'Will Do'*<br>▪ *On those occasions where the team member has greater 'expert' knowledge than the Leader*<br>▪ *Where the team member is capable of solving problems alone but sometimes needs encouragement and reassurance to feel confident in facing tough challenge*<br>▪ *When the team member has sufficient competence and Will to try things our for self*<br>▪ *Where the operating culture is already a 'collegiate', one such is often the case with professional or knowledgeable workers, where the requirement on the Leader is to be first amongst equals* |
| **Tips in Applying the Mentoring Style** | ▪ *Don't mistake control for accountability; because the Leader is accountable for overall decisions, it does not mean Control and Command*<br>▪ *Work to encourage team member's confidence in their own decisions, don't undermine them by suggesting you could always do it better*<br>▪ *To learn making mistakes occasionally, except where carelessness is involved treat mistakes as learning opportunities*<br>▪ *Be more delighted when they can do it without you than when they need you (although always support willingly); your ego is less important than your team member's success.* |

<table>
<tr><th colspan="2">4. ENABLING</th></tr>
<tr><td>Characteristics of Enabling</td><td>This is not abdication, but a conscious clear recognition by the Leader that with a particular piece of work, at least, the team member can do it, by themselves, to a standard that is expert. The team member owns that part of the work, makes the decisions, is involved in it, is entrusted and empowered to make their own judgement and to use initiative responsibly. The Leader withdraws from the operations part of the work, but with a firm understanding that the team member will keep him/her appropriately informed. The Leader does not withdraw their support, however; the challenge belongs to the team member but the Leader continues to provide strong, visible support in the background. It matters still to the Leader that the team member is successful, more so than ever.<br>▪ The Leader leaves the team member completely free to deal with issues and make decisions for a particular piece of work, within an overall framework of parameters such as safety, budget requirements, etc<br>▪ Although the Leader does not require to be involved, s/he will require to be kept appropriately informed , such as with issues that impact other work, and to maintain their view of the big picture<br>▪ The Leader will still seek opportunities to recognise achievement and to maintain the relationship of support and encouragement</td></tr>
<tr><td>When to use the Enabling Style</td><td>▪ Where there is both high 'Can Do' and 'Will Do' in a particular job area<br>▪ To arrange more of the same<br>▪ As a reward for those who demonstrate competence and willingness, and who are strongly motivated, intrinsically, to do good work<br>▪ When the Leader can usefully direct his/her own time to other important issues</td></tr>
</table>

| | |
|---|---|
| **When to use the Enabling Style** *continued* | ▪ *When the requirements of the task are best suited to this style, eg customer service where each service opportunity needs to be tailored, within an overall framework, to the unique characteristics of the situation* |
| **Tips in Applying the Enabling Style** | ▪ *Judge when the team member is ready for this style and tell them that they will take full charge of the piece of work from now on. You will have succeeded when you have enabled someone to operate in an enabled way*<br>▪ *Give the team member the car keys, so to speak, but prize your own fingers off the steering wheel; don't interfere*<br>▪ *If the team member asks too often, at first, for help, consciously push the decision back to them by asking what they would do*<br>▪ *Accept that the team members approach might be different from yours, this doesn't mean that the results will be worse, they might even be better*<br>▪ *Deal with mistakes productively and take accountability for them; mistakes will happen. Don't stop yourself from enabling others by your own timidity, you'll be stuck on an activity treadmill for ever if you do*<br>▪ *Find opportunities to stay in contact with the team member without getting involved in the detail of what they are doing* |

# Assessing Development Levels for Particular Tasks

At any particular time each team member, and also the team as a whole, will be at a particular stage of development for a particular task. It is important to be clear about what stage they are at so that you can be Situationally Consistent in the way you deal with them and also prepare for the next stage ahead.

The Development Level has two major components:

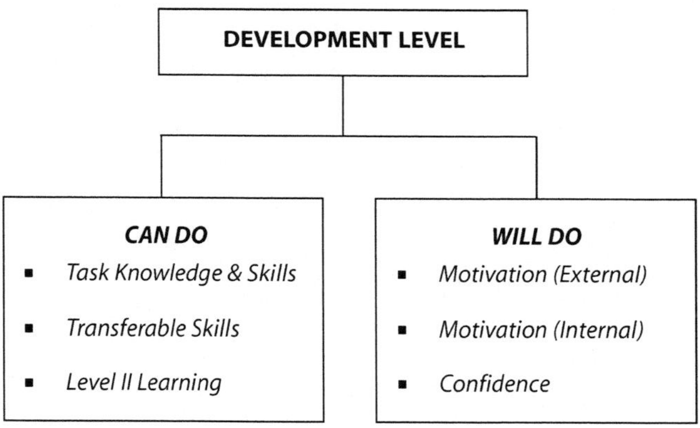




When combined in varying amounts Can Do and Will Do can be experienced as four levels of development for the particular task ranging from low, when the Directing Style is appropriate, to high, when the Enabling style fits better.

In many ways the Directing and Coaching Styles are 'Push' ones while the Mentoring and Enabling Styles are 'Pull' ones. The crossover point, and what the Leader/Developer is seeking to achieve, is the switch to Intrinsic Motivation and its corresponding dynamic of Level II learning. This is the Transformational Stage, as has been described, where energy and commitment become their most powerful and what the most effective Leader/Developers always work towards.

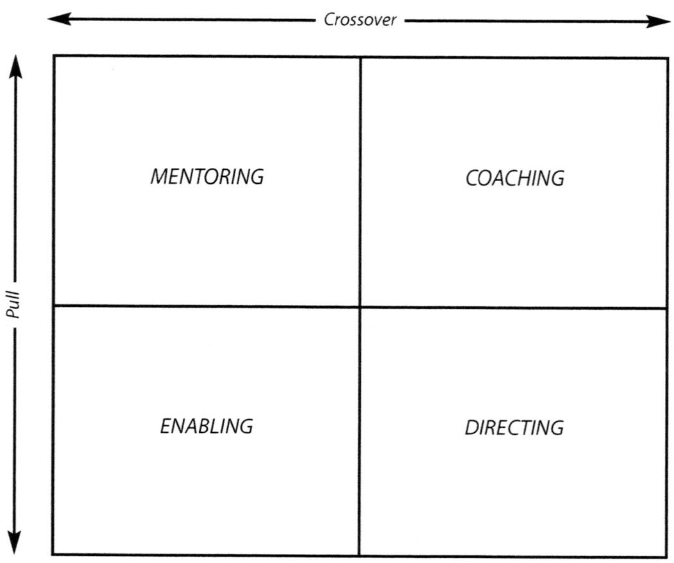


In developing people through this approach a number of points are especially important:

- *It is the Will Do that is the Motivation, which is often the most important aspect as Skills and Knowledge are usually more readily trainable*
- *When the Will Do becomes "I Really Want To" - that is, the Motivation comes from within the person themselves and not through some external reward or avoidance of consequences; Level II Learning really comes into its own and provides the continuing impetus; Commitment is much stronger than Compliance*
- *Getting the balance right between putting too much on the team member before they can handle it, and thus setting them up for failure and frustration, or holding them back from stretching their wings, so to speak, is crucial - both can be equally damaging*
- *Sometimes it will be necessary to revert back a step before starting to move the process forward again, either because the person wasn't quite ready or because they are not maintaining the new performance level*

# Assessing Levels of Development Maturity

A useful way of reviewing someone's Development Level at a particular task is to use the Maturity Matrix below:

*Developed* ← *Maturity* → *Developing*

| HIGH | GOOD | MODERATE | LOW |
|---|---|---|---|
| ↓ *High Can Do* | ↓ *Good Can Do* | ↓ *Moderate Can Do* | ↓ *Low Can Do* |
| *High Will Do* ↓ | *High Will Do* *(but perhaps lacking in confidence)* ↓ | *Moderate to High Will Do* ↓ | *Low to High Will Do* ↓ |
| ENABLING | MENTORING | COACHING | DIRECTING |

*Pull* ↕ (left) — *Push* ↕ (right)

← *Appropriate Style* →



Ask yourself the following questions when assessing the present state of the person, or teams, Can Do and Will Do.

| CAN DO | WILL DO |
|---|---|
| ▪ Do they understand what is required and that it is part of their job?<br>▪ Have they received the appropriate training?<br>▪ Do they have the skills and knowledge required?<br>▪ Have they done the task successfully before?<br>▪ Are they a Level I or a Level II Learner? | ▪ Do they want to learn how to do the task?<br>▪ Are they willing to take on the task?<br>▪ Is there something 'in it' for them?<br>▪ Are they prepared to accept responsibility for the result?<br>▪ Are they a Level I or Level II Learner?<br>▪ Do they have the confidence to try out the task? |

You can then readily assess the current stage of development for the particular task by using the Matrix.

# Chapter Summary

- *No one Style is effective in all situations. Effective Leader/Developers flex their style appropriately in response to, or cause, a particular situation, but they do so consistently.*
- *The appropriateness of the Style used is based on:*
  - *the ability of the Leader to select the right Style for the situation (Style Effectiveness), and to use an appropriate range of Styles matched to the situation (Style Flexibility). When applied consistently, this gives rise to Situational Consistency*
  - *doing this well – which requires an understanding of the individual and their 'maturity' in terms of Can Do and Will Do for a particular task.*
- *There are four basic Styles – Directing, Coaching, Mentoring and Enabling – all of which require Support, but different expressions of this for each.*



- *Most Leader/Developers have one or two Primary Preferred Styles. It is useful to know what your bias is so that you can 'round out' your repertoire.*
- *Flexing your Style to match someone's increasing job 'maturity' is one form of Reward for them; equally, flexing Style can be used as a Penalty or Consequence.*
- ***Performance = (Can Do x Will Do) Situation***

  *In this, the Situational Factors matter greatly, and it is the Leader/Developer who defines the situation. Effective Leader/Developers create the situation for the team's success.*
- *Transformational Leaders motivate us to do more than we originally expected we could do. They are skilled Mentors and Enablers.*
- *In many ways, the Directing and Coaching Styles are 'push' ones, while the Mentoring and Enabling Styles are 'pull' ones as these involve Level II Learning and the engagement of Intrinsic Motivation.*
- *Reviewing someone's present development level, and thus matching your Style appropriately, is much aided by using the Maturity Matrix.*
- *Remember that all Styles require High Support, including the Enabling one.*

# chapter 10

# Leading Change & Transition

- *Planned Change and Leading & Developing High Performance*
  - *Incremental and Step Change*
  - *Challenge and Support in Leading Change Mastery*
- *The Change Transition Curve*
  - *The Stages of the Curve*
- *Attitudes to Change*
- *The Marathon Effect*
- *Change and Performance Gain (or Loss)*
  - *Performance Curve – Potential Gains (or Loss)*
  - *What is Good Change Leadership?*
- *Preparing Yourself to Lead Change*
- *Intensity of Effort*
- *Checklist – 'How to deal with change"*
- *Chapter Summary*

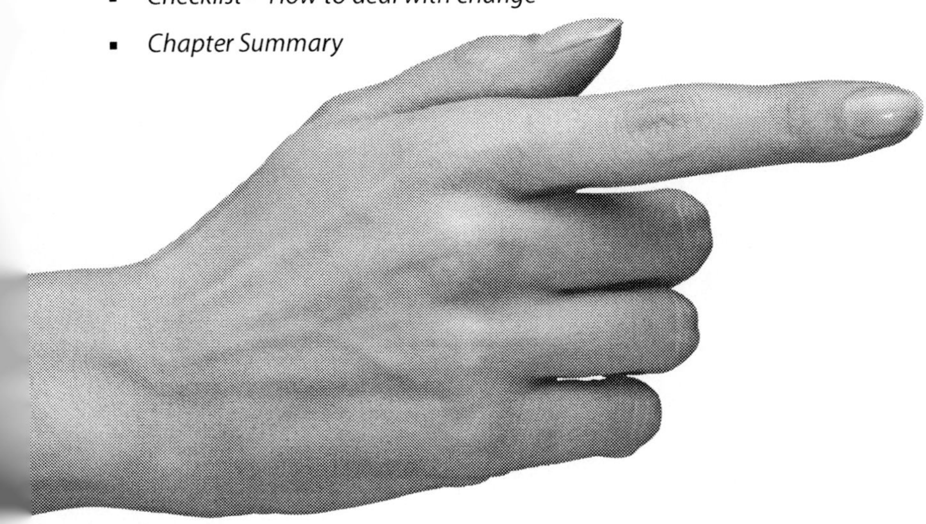

# Planned Change and Leading & Developing High Performance

Leading & Developing High Performance is concerned with bringing about necessary and planned change. Planned in that it is visioned and led, through the process and stages described, as a series of digestible stages - sometimes called Incremental Change or Continuous Improvement. It is necessary because, in today's world, High Performance is the route to both personal and organisational survival. One of the features of High Performance Teams is that they deal with change with vigour and resolution, as a new Challenge, buttressed by Support, confident and capable of doing what is required.

It is not surprising that such teams respond this way for they have acquired, through the actions of the Leader/Developer, the habits of being enabled, Continuous Improvement, Level II Learning and the ability to use their initiative, responsibly. Organisational change, almost inevitably, is in the direction of these skills and habits, which are themselves the ingredients of successful adaptation and growth. Leader/Developers who secure such High Performance Teams are not only dealing with today's needs, but preparing for those of tomorrow. For change is inevitable and certain, and those people and organisations who cope best with it have become well versed in its 'rules of engagement' and know they have the capacity to cope.



The last decade, or so, has been a decade of change for most organisations, and that change has often been turbulent rather than the more incremental approach of yesteryear. The future, too, is not as predictable as it once seemed to be. The only certainty is that there will be further waves of change, just as sea waves roll in from beyond the horizon – some gentle, others threatening, with the occasional unpredictable rogue wave, larger and more devastating than the rest.

Some organisations, and individuals within them, have 'surfed' such waves of change well, harnessing their power and energy, while others have bobbed about in the backwash like jetsam. Still others, denying the existence of such waves, turned their back to them only to receive a cold, sharp shock when a wave, larger than the rest, caught them unawares.

Change, whether it be incremental or step, is likely to continue. Managing in a constantly changing environment requires the new competencies we have talked about, that are radically different in surviving and prospering in today's world.

## Incremental and Step Change

Incremental, continuous change, generally speaking, works better than step change, and incremental, continuous change (sometimes called Transformational Change) comes through the Leading & Developing High Performance processes which have been described. Sometimes though, the situation or the organisation requires a step change which is larger and more sudden than an incremental approach. Typically, step change is large scale and organisation wide, such as:

- *Downsizing – 'cutting out the fat'*
- *Flattening the Structure – eliminating middle management positions*
- *Decentralising corporate staff functions*
- *Introducing a 'new' culture*
- *Business Process Re-engineering*



However, the Leading & Developing High Performance principles and processes still apply, often more strongly than ever, because....

- *Change means new Competencies (Skills and Behaviours) which have to be accepted, developed and mastered*
- *Explicitness in what is required helps enormously (remember the story about roller skating on top of a tall building in the dark?)*
- *Every change will have some spin-off of unintended consequences which will need to be spotted and dealt with*
- *High Challenge (which is how change can be interpreted) will lead to stress and random development and performance unless accompanied by High Support.*

## Challenge and Support in Leading Change Mastery

The last point deserves particular emphasis because there is a process we all go through when encountering change, whether it be a new job or whether we need to respond to a new situation of change. Sometimes it is a matter of days before people effect the transition, sometimes years, sometimes people get stuck and never successfully complete the transition (which is painful and debilitating). Also people go through the process at different rates, or can regress, which can be confusing for the Leader/Developer. The Leader/Developer has a key role in all this by providing the Support necessary, but the kind of Support required will vary according to what stage of the process the person has reached.

# The Change Transition Curve

The process, or Transition Curve, is shown below, with the two axes being the feeling of Competence/Morale (being able to cope / a preparedness to make the effort to cope) and Time. Feelings matter a great deal when people are moving through the Transition Curve and, as well as labelling each stage with a one word description of behaviour, the underlying mindset (using the language of the OK Corral described earlier) has also been included.

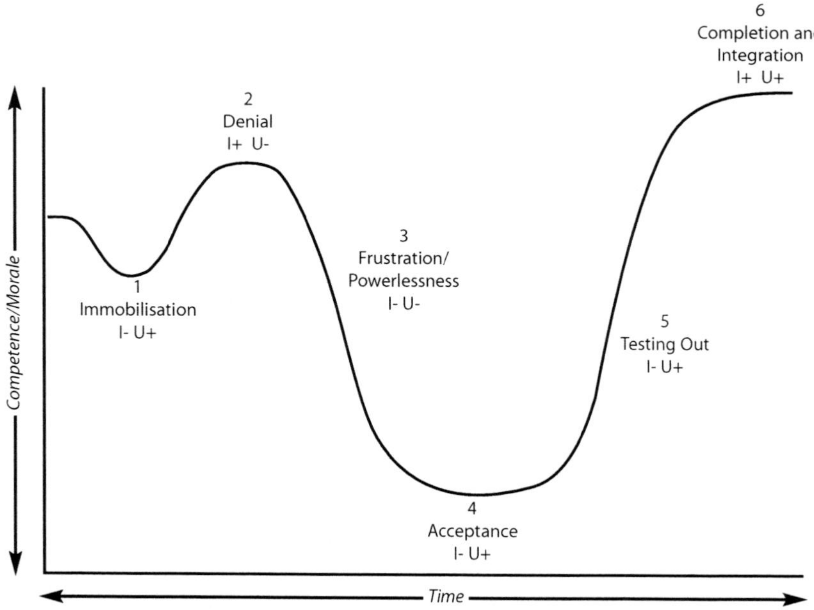




From a personal point of view, whilst understanding and accepting this natural reaction does not affect the change, it does help us to cope and rise to the challenges presented by the change more productively.

This understanding also makes our dealings with others who are experiencing change, and who are therefore on the curve, more supportive and helps them survive and thrive.

**The Stages of the Curve:**

Stage 1 is typified by shock, temporary disbelief and a sense of paralysis. Even a positive change can elicit this response - in the sense of not believing your good luck. Imagine the response of a winner in the National Lottery!

Stage 2 represents the individual's attempts to shrug off the change and continue as if nothing had happened, a denial that they are affected by the change. It is possible for some people to get stuck at this stage, in which case the wave of change will eventually swamp them.

Stage 3 is the downward slope. It is an inevitable and necessary stage during which people can experience a whole range of emotions, such as grief, rage, fear, etc. Behaviour can be irrational and this is not a time to make major decisions. To help someone who is experiencing this stage, it is best to just support and accept the feelings - logic has little use here.

Stage 4 Eventually the emotion of Stage 3 gives way to an acceptance of the situation. The person can feel drained and resigned, but see the need to get on with it. Help from others, particularly the Leader/Developer, is essential at this stage to begin the rebuilding process.

Stage 5 represents the testing of new approaches and behaviours and the inevitable learning that comes from mistakes accepted and built upon. This is the time to encourage the person to take a few risks and to test out alternatives.

Stage 6 is the return to effective operation. Behaviours and Attitudes have shifted and integrated into a way of life. It is significant to note that the level of competence at Stage 6 is higher than at the start of the curve, as the process of transition leads to personal growth and a better ability to cope with future change.

# Attitudes to Change

It is interesting to overlay our attitude to ourselves and others (OK Corral Model) to the Transition Curve. This is particularly important when we need to deal with others experiencing change, and whose behaviours seem at odds with their 'normal' approach. By reflecting on this model, we can better assist their progress through the curve and thus help them achieve integration more readily.

At Stage 2 it is likely that the attitude to the world, and particularly towards the perceived perpetrators of the change, will be one of I'm OK - You're not OK. People will seek to blame others and react with aggression and resistance to the situation.

By Stage 3 they are likely to have shifted and have occupied the I'm not OK - You're not OK quadrant on the OK Corral Model. They can be suspicious and hostile, whilst harbouring all sorts of doubts and fears about their own ability to cope, and about their future.



Provided they reach Stage 4 with some evidence of Support around them, their attitude will once again shift. This time to one of I'm not OK - You're OK, typified by continuing self doubts, but with a belief that others may have the answer. From the Leader/Developer's position, it is necessary to firmly demonstrate I'm OK - You're OK behaviours to prevent them becoming dependent and stuck in the I-U+ mode.

> *Encouragement ... Recognition ... Confidence Building*
> *are all very helpful in assisting people to fully achieve the transition*

During this time the Leader/Developer will be on the receiving end of behaviours from the person going through the transition, some of it aggressive and hostile, at other times passive or alienated. The golden rule is for the Leader to stay in the I+U+ position, not reacting to hostility, powerlessness, etc, but recognising where people are in the process and maintaining Positive Regard and Support for them.

When someone starts to move from Stage 3 to 4 for example, the Leader must be ready for them because, in effect, the person is holding out a hand and saying "help". Leaders need to spot and action this, albeit tentative, request for help, as they have earned the right to be asked by the Support provided in the earlier Stages. Finally, as previously mentioned, it essential that Leaders don't cause the other person to become always dependent on them, but rather that they are enabled to become fully competent and complete the transition.

# The Marathon Effect

By the time the elite runners in the London Marathon are finishing, some runners have only just started their race. They may start very slowly and take lots of rests along the way. The elite runners, on the other hand, are well prepared, run to their own pace, and when they cross the line they start planning their next event.

It is easy for Leader/Developers to forget this 'marathon' effect when dealing with change. At their best, Leader/Developers will have completed their own transitions before the rest of the team get started; they are like the elite runners. If you do not manage your own transition through the transition curve process ahead of the team, then you will hardly be in a position to Support team members, whether they are 'hares' or 'tortoises'. You cannot help others unless you are 'in shape' yourself. You may have experienced or led change before and know what to expect; you may have, rightly, trained hard and prepared yourself so you are better positioned to cope than many of your team members.



Hopefully, you will not take on the arrogance of 'I'm OK – You're Not OK', too often displayed by new Leaders appointed to rescue or change an existing team and who are dismissive about the difficulties some team members may have in catching up with them.

Not everyone runs at the same pace and, whether hares or tortoises, crossing the finishing line and completing the transition process in the best possible speed, for them, is what matters. In this the Leader/Developer has an enormous influence, but only if they can provide the Challenge and Support needed by individuals as individuals, recognising where each person is on the transition curve at each step of the way, thus providing the Change Leadership necessary. To do this well requires the Leader/Developer to be well ahead in their own transition, without forgetting the road s/he has travelled to get there.

# Change and Performance Gain (or Loss)

Many, if not most, step changes do not result in the effectiveness gains their organisations had envisaged. Some of this is due to the time and effort it takes to achieve effective implementation, some because the required change in behaviour required never really happens, except at lip service level.

During step change, performance parallels the transition curve (or coping cycle) as shown below. It will be noticed that it is, paradoxically, at the 'Letting Go' stage, where a break through is poised to happen, that performance is often at its lowest ebb.

***Change and Performance Gain (or Loss) Curve***

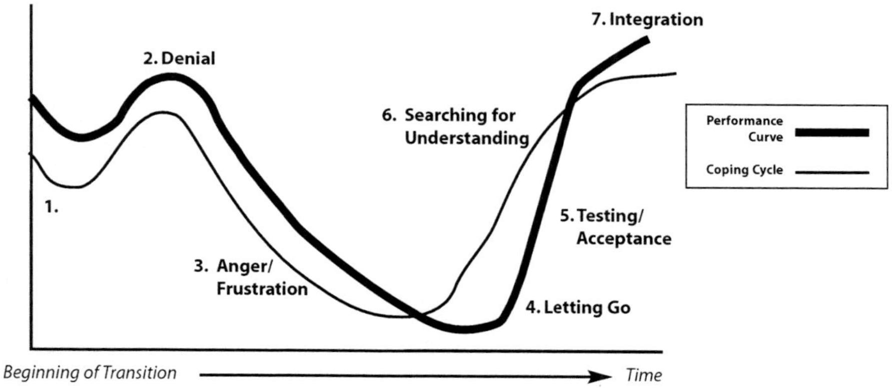




The Performance Curve and the Transition one can vary along both the axes of Performance and Time. **It depends, to very large measure, on the Leader/Developer, for change needs to be led and led well.** It also involves developing people, as new approaches, skills and behaviours are always involved.

A situation which is not led well can result in low performance, over a long period of time, while effecting a change which is well led will result in high performance, in a much shorter time, with much less stress for the people concerned. The potential effectiveness/productivity gains, or losses, are significant, as is the amount of pain suffered or not. This can be shown diagrammatically, as follows:

*Performance Curve – Potential Gains (or Loss)*

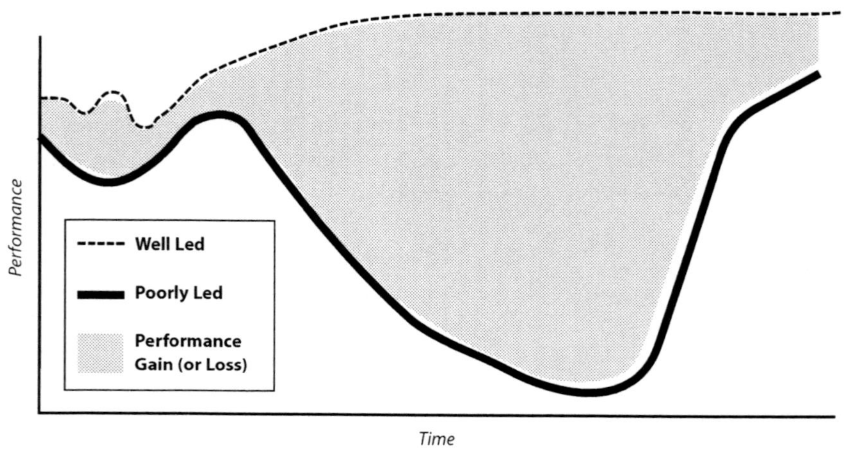




## What is Good Change Leadership?

It is simply the approach, process and skills we have described, applied in a particular context and in an intensive way, which places additional demands on the Leader/Developer. In many ways it is concerned with accelerating the process, not just with the transactional part of building people's skills, but also with the transformational one of enabling new attitudes and behaviour. For most step change involves a change in the culture of 'the way things are done around here' involving a different approach to doing the job in the direction of people being more enabled and operating at a higher level of personal effectiveness.

The core of all this, and the central part of good Change Leadership, is the High Challenge/High Support approach. Again, it is both/and not either/or. Without both High Challenge and High Support, successful, enduring change is very unlikely to be well implemented. Understanding the transition curve process will enable Support, and Challenge, to be appropriately used.

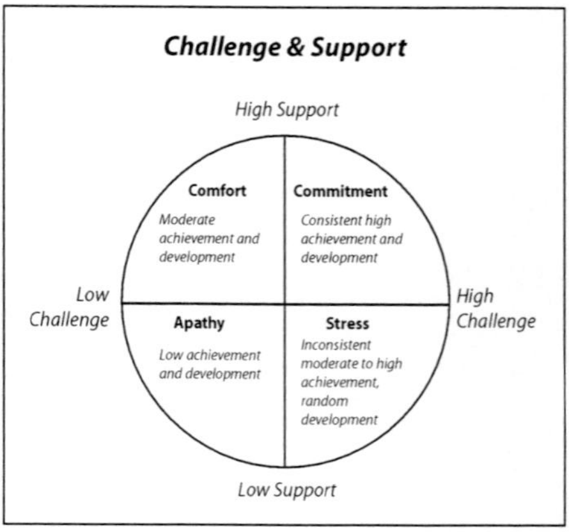

# Preparing Yourself to Lead Change

There is a saying that goes 'You cannot help others unless you are in good shape yourself'. In situations of step change this applies particularly to the Leader/Developer. Furthermore, there is an intensity of effort required by the Leader/Developer which, unless s/he is in good shape, cannot be sustained. For the Leader/Developer is the role model to the team in coping with change, and what s/he does well, or poorly, will have an exaggerated effect.

This means that you, as the Leader/Developer, need to be through the transition process ahead of your team, or at least a stage or two ahead of them. Dealing with someone who is at the Shock or Denial stage will be much harder, for them as well as for you, if you yourself are on the 'downward slope' of anger or frustration. Letting Go or Testing/Acceptance is the minimum place you must be before you can start to help, rather than just collude with others.



Be aware that you will need your own source of support – this is a reality, no matter how 'tough' you are, and if your boss doesn't provide this, you will have to find someone else you can talk things through with occasionally, outside your team.

Much will depend on whether you can commit to the new situation; if you cannot, another reality is that your working life will be frustrating and stressful, and you won't be in a position to Lead or to Develop. A crucial part of this process is, again, Visioning – what will it be like when the change is implemented and working well? This will give you the future direction we talked about earlier, and also the resilience and reduction in stress which comes with goal clarity. You are also then in a position to sign on, to commit to it, or not, as well as to model what is required.

# Intensity of Effort

The difference between Leading & Developing High Performance and Leading Step Change is one of degree more than anything else. The principles and practices are the same – what varies is that step change is usually a more accelerated process, requiring a greater intensity of effort by the Leader/Developer. Additionally, the Leader/Developer has to raise their own game, to use more the skills and principles of developing high performance, to be rock solid in leading from the mindset of High Challenge/High Support and generally to be more active and involved. And all of this when there are likely to be greater demands on him or her anyway. So what is the secret?

There is no secret. We end by completing the circle. For what we have explored together is an approach as a way of life, and a process set of competencies that go beyond 'mere management' and which are necessary to secure your own and your team's success in today's and tomorrow's world. They are necessary anyway as part of your everyday working life and, if you apply and polish them as part of this everyday working life, you will not only harvest great benefits for you and your team, but you are also preparing yourself to cope with change.



Such step change will come, and will come and come again, but like the athlete who is prepared, you will have the fitness and resources to cope with it well, while perhaps others and their teams are floundering.

This is the Challenge to you, to become a more effective Leader/Developer today, and equip yourself by absorbing the skills we have described, so that they become second nature, requiring only a touch on the accelerator when step change inevitably comes along.

How fit are you at present? The following checklist will give you some indication as well as reviewing, for you, how far you have travelled on our journey together, and what you will need to do to complete that journey.

# Checklist – "How I Deal With Change"

Method

The following statements relate to how you deal with change. Please indicate which answer best relates to you by ticking the appropriate box. Then consider your responses so you know where to focus additional effort.

| In Managing Change I .................. | | Always | Often | Sometimes | Rarely |
|---|---|---|---|---|---|
| 1 | am consistent, my actions match my words and people know what I stand for | | | | |
| 2 | talk with my people and genuinely listen to their ideas or difficulties | | | | |
| 3 | maintain a future perspective and goal direction, not allowing myself to be swamped by confusion | | | | |
| 4 | project a clear vision of the future to my team and transmit my enthusiasm for and commitment to it | | | | |
| 5 | provide clarity about what needs to be done | | | | |
| 6 | make difficult/unpopular decisions or apply strong leadership when necessary, and take ownership of the outcomes | | | | |
| 7 | give strong feedback to help individuals achieve what is now required and reinforce progress | | | | |
| 8 | resiliently pursue my overall direction while not being thrown off course by setbacks and difficulties | | | | |
| 9 | identify accurately the reasons why an individual has difficulties in coping with the change, and generate solutions | | | | |
| 10 | flex my style appropriately to deal with varying levels of progress to what is required and a person's position on the transition curve | | | | |
| 11 | am highly perceptive to individual needs and motivation, and treat people as individuals | | | | |
| 12 | accept mistakes will happen in trying new ways and treat such mistakes as part of the learning process | | | | |
| 13 | actively build each team member's capability, will and confidence to deal with the change required | | | | |
| 14 | create the situation where my team not only reach new job mastery and self-directing behaviours to meet the change successfully, but are more equipped to deal with future change | | | | |
| 15 | always maintain strong support and encouragement to help my team meet the new challenge | | | | |

# Chapter Summary

- *A major benefit of the Leading & Developing High Performance approach is that it prepares people to deal with inevitable change.*
- *Continuous Improvement or Incremental Change generally works better than Step Change.*
- *Change means new Competencies (Skills and Behaviours) have to be accepted, developed and mastered.*
- *Every change will have some unintended consequences which will need to be spotted and dealt with.*
- *High Challenge Change, unless underpinned by High Support, will lead to stress and random development.*
- *People go through a process – the Transition Curve – when experiencing significant change. They complete this process at different rates.*
- *Some people get 'stuck' in the process and need practical help.*
- *Knowing the process and the Stage someone is at helps enormously in supporting that person to move on to the next Stage.*
- *Successful change rarely happens by itself – it is led.*
- *The Leadership required demands the same Attitudes and Skills as those for Leading & Developing High Performance.*
- *To effect successful change, as Leader/Developer you must be ahead of your team on the Transition Curve and be actively using the skills and principles of developing high performance.*

# postscript

## Putting It All Together

- *Putting It All Together*
- *'The Competency Wheel'*

# Putting It All Together

Charismatic heroes need not apply! What we have described lies well within the gift of most managers. Whether you are an already established manager with many years experience who wants to review and up-date your skills, or someone about to become responsible for the work of others for the first time, we wish you well.

The 'mystique' to Leading & Developing High Performance isn't a mystique at all really, but a readily understandable and accessible process. It is not to do with who you are, but what you believe in and what you do. What you believe in is central to all; it is the hub of your wheel of skills and, without this solid hub, the spokes of skills will buckle, and the wheel will not carry you and your team forward. These central beliefs, or mindset, are the **both/and** ones of *High Challenge* **and** *High Support*, held in equal and powerful combination, and reinforced by Positive Regard, Genuineness and High Expectations (see page 212).



The Process of Leading & Developing High Performance gives a path to run on; a coherent and practical direction to follow. Within this Process there are a number of skills, and here we have concentrated on the less well known ones, as others, such as questioning and listening, are more commonly available. Again, there is nothing magical about the skills required; what we have tried to do is to make them accessible to you in a digestible, useable form. We are also not advocating just one technique, such as coaching for example, for the reality is that you will be dealing with a range of people all at different stages of development and with different needs. So you must be prepared to deal with A-Z, so to speak, but all within the same direction and purpose.

The purpose starts with the underlying attitudes you have, as the Leader/Developer, and your own clear vision for your team. You can then identify any team and individual changes required in specific, behavioural terms, diagnosing why the performance issue is occurring and what rewards and penalties are part of the equation.

Start the process of giving strong feedback and reinforce each improvement step by 'catching them doing it right'. It is a little and often process, but one where maintaining momentum is crucial, as well as maintaining your own resilience. For if you are dealing with entrenched and habituated behaviours, to make the progress you desire, you will need to work firstly through the Mobilising Stage.

During this time you will start to become aware of individual differences in motivation patterns, and tailor your approach to connect with individual needs, without losing sight of your situational consistency. Or perhaps your people are already at the stage where it is appropriate to flex your style, starting the Developing and Enabling stages of the Process through to a Coaching or Mentoring style, operating more in a transformational than a transactional way, and encouraging Level II Learning fuelled by intrinsic motivation.

Keep faith with your overall vision of enabling your people to become 'the best they can be', and for many this will involve journeying from dependence through to interdependence, being self-directing in their use of Responsible Initiative, as well as having professional mastery for a particular task – that is, they can be fully delegated and empowered.

## The Competency Wheel

The same principles apply to two special applications, unlocking team potential through harnessing the power of the team, and in Leading the inevitable change transition. Inevitable because change will always occur – the only certainty – and leading and developing your team in the way we have suggested will best equip them to cope well and succeed with it.

This continuous process is a voyage where you are the navigator. The continuous improvement will apply to you too. How well equipped are you for this voyage? Look at the competencies? again (for Leading & Developing High Performance and assess where now you feel you should put your own development energies, and action this – prepare yourself for the voyage!

"Bon Voyage"

# bibliography


Alderfer, C P — Existence, Relatedness & Growth, New York Free Press 1972

Bass, B — Leadership & Performance Beyond Expectations, The Free Press, NY 1985

Bass, B — From Transactional to Transformational Leadership, Organisational Dynamics 18, 1990

Biddle, D & Evendon, R — Human Aspects of Management, IPM 1989

Blake, R & Mouton, J — The New Managerial Grid, Gulf Publishing 1985

Berne, E — Games People Play, Ballantine 1978

Dilts, Robert B — Visioning Leadership Skills, Meta Publications, 1996

Hamner, W C — Reinforcement Theory – Organisation Behaviour & Management, Clair Press 1974

Handy, C — Understanding Organisations, Penguin 1986

Hamill, A — Unpublished papers

Hersey, P — The Situational Leader, Warner Books, NY 1984

Hersey, P & Blanchard, K — Management of Organizational Behaviour, Pearson Higher Education 1988

Herzberg, F — The Gold & Garbage in Management Theories, Ohio University Press 1980

Hofstede, G — Cultural Contraints in Management Theories, University of Limburg, Maastricht, 1993

House, R — A Theory of Charismatic Leadership

Maslow, A — Motivation & Personality, Harper & Row 1970

McGregor, D — The Human Side of Enterprise, McGraw Hill 1960

Moss Kanter, R — When Giants Learn to Dance, International Thomson Business Press 1992

Nadler, D & Lawler, E — Motivation & Diagnostic Approach, Perspective on Behaviour in Organisations, McGraw Hill 1977

Peters, T & Waterman, R — In Search of Excellence, Harper & Row 1982

Reddin, W F — The 3D Management Style Theory, Training & Development Journal 21, 1967

Schein, E H — Organisation Culture & Leadership, Jossey-Bass 1988

Schein, E H — Career Dynamics, Matching Individual and Organisational Needs, Addison Wesley 1978

Senge, P — The Fifth Discipline, Doubleday, NY 1980

Skinner, B — Beyond Freedom & Dignity, Hackett Publishing Company 1971

Stewart I & Joines V — TA Today, Lifespace Publishing

Toffler A — The Third Wave, Barton Books 1980

Wagner, A — The Transactional Manager, Prentice Hall 1981

# theories explained

**McGregor**

The background to McGregor's work was his realisation that organisations and managers within them viewed motivation from a set of assumptions about employees (what we have called here a mindset or underlying values). At that the time there were two predominant sets.

1. Those based on the 'Scientific Management' School of Frederic Taylor et al. Here managers determined the most efficient way to perform tasks, the carrying out of which was rewarded by wage incentives. The underlying assumptions were that managers understood the work better than workers, who were essentially lazy and who could only be motivated by money. 'Thinking' (the managers) was separated from 'Doing' (the workers). This we have called the Command and Control approach, and which, in terms of human capital, neglected the view that 'with every pair of hands comes a free brain'.

   Taylorism worked best where work was repetitive, and did give rise to enormous productivity gains during the era of initial mass production. However, it soon became apparent that it had many flaws, that it often reduced motivation, generated uncooperative attitudes to put it mildly, and that workers had more complex needs than those assumed.

2. Those based on the 'Human Relations' School of Elton Mayo et al. The researchers found that boredom reduced motivation, that employees set group norms about the level of work they thought was right, that social contact and attention had a positive effect. Thus, instead of workers being expected to accept management's authority simply in return for wages, an emphasis was put on the acceptance of authority through treating people with consideration and allowing more participation.

McGregor identified two different sets of assumptions, positioned at the ends of a continuum, that managers have about the people they manage:

- ***Theory X*** *– where people have an inherent dislike of work and will avoid it whenever possible, and prefer to avoid responsibility and self direction. They can tolerate it if the pay is decent and the boss fair and considerate. Thus people must be closely supervised and controlled at work, and detailed procedures and routines established.*

  *Interestingly McGregor saw the Human Relations School as simply a more sophisticated version of Theory X.*

- ***Theory Y*** *– where work is as natural as play or rest, that in fact people want to work and, under the right circumstances, derive a great deal of satisfaction from it. People have the capacity to accept and even seek responsibility and self directedness, and to apply creativity to solving problems for themselves.*

Before moving on it is worth pointing out that often managers hold two models simultaneously, one for themselves (Y) and another for their subordinates!

McGregor recognised that at the time the way work was organised did not give much scope for Y, work being organised largely on a (Tofler*) second wave basis. However, it is now, through economic necessity, largely based on a third wave one, where operating in the direction of assumption Y is arguably a necessity to meet modern patterns of work and organisational survival.

| **Changes in Work Organisation** | |
|---|---|
| **First Wave**<br>eg Weaving<br>Small-holding | ▪ *Self sufficiency*<br>▪ *Cottage industry*<br>▪ *Craftsman approach*<br>▪ *Local focus* |
| **Second Wave**<br>eg Mass production | ▪ *Economies of scale*<br>▪ *Specialisation /producing small parts*<br>▪ *De-skilling*<br>▪ *Hierarchical decision making* |
| **Third Wave**<br>eg Customer service Flexibility | ▪ *Decentralisation*<br>▪ *Flatter hierarchies*<br>▪ *Customer responsiveness*<br>▪ *Professionalisation*<br>▪ *Interdependence* |

Also, McGregor did not see X or Y as either/or except as a way of labelling managers' assumptions about people. In fact he subsequently argued the both/and view of Theory Z, based on people being a mixture of both.

How does this fit with the underlying assumptions of High Challenge High Support? Firstly High Challenge Low Support can be seen as a version of X, as can Low Challenge High Support. In its intent High Challenge High Support fits closest with Theory Y, but, and this is an important but, recognises that Z holds good in that people can be in differing starting positions or stages of development. For example, some people may have become habituated to being treated in a Theory X way, also some managers cling on to operating this way because it is what they have learned.

In this loose sense Y is the meta vision, but Z is the way it is achieved through recognising the differences in people and where they are at, working forward one step at a time. In this sense transactional skills are required more in the direction of X, and transformational ones aligned more to Y.

## Maslow

Maslow's theory of Motivation is probably the most widely known of all the motivation theories since it classifies human needs in an logical, convenient way. Although, arguably, the needs apply to the vast majority of people, they do so with different intensities and requirements, eg one person may have a higher need for security than another and equally two people may value different ways of meeting their self esteem needs.

Today's thinking is that for people in work, physiological needs and security needs are largely met, although there is now an argument that maintains that security is more to do with employability than being employed (Moss Kanter). This in itself has much to do with competence and being able to operate independently/interdependently skills and mindsets supported by the High Challenge High Support approach.

Next in the hierarchy is the need to belong, perhaps most strongly felt outside work, but an important need inside work too. Unless people feel they are an integral part of the organisation, they are unlikely to respond to so called higher order needs.

Maslow described two types of self esteem needs – achievement and competence – to be good at the job and also status and recognition, achieving something important when performing the job, which has meaning. Equally for some, with self actualisation, new responsibilities and personal growth will matter, while for others producing work of high quality will, while for yet others developing useful, creative ideas fulfils the same need. Maslow points out that individual differences are greatest at this level, which is why, if we accept that mastering performance excellence is about enabling people to operate at Maslow's Self Esteem and Actualising levels, a deeper and more pragmatic understanding, such as might be gained through the Motivation Inventory, about individual motivation patterns is useful.

Maslow has been criticised for seeming to suggest that his Hierarchy of Needs is applicable across all cultures. Hofstede discovered, not surprisingly, great variation among cultures, which he ascribed to differences in 'collective mental programming' based on a specific value system. For example, he found that in Sweden social needs are valued over esteem needs, while in Gemrany and Japan security was generally valued over social and esteem needs. In France, security needs are highly valued but so are social ones. In the UK, Canada, India and the USA of course where Maslow's work was carried out, Maslow's theory applied relatively well. Additionally there will be cultural variations within nation states, as well as between them.

Alderfer reached broadly similar views to Maslow but with some important differences in two basic ways. Firstly Alderfer saw the hierarchy in just three categories:

> **Existence needs** – similar to Maslow's physiological needs, but extended beyond a survival level to include, for example, fringe benefits
>
> **Relatedness needs** – for interpersonal relationships, similar to Maslow's Belonging
>
> **Growth needs** – for personal creativity and influence, again similar to Maslow's Self Esteem and Actualisation

….. the whole being known as ERG Theory. The second important difference from Maslow is that while Maslow saw people moving steadily up the hierarchy of needs, Alderfer argued people moved up and down the hierarchy from time to time and from situation to situation, which fits the perception and experience of many practicing managers. Important in this is that if efforts to reach one level of needs are frustrated, individuals will regress (maybe in a bruised, frustrated manner) to a lower level which hits their expectations as to what is possible.

Both theories offer useful insights, but are perhaps too broad to operationalise when treating people as individuals in terms of identifying and meeting their particular differences and needs. The overall direction they are suggesting however, are very much supportive of the aims of transformational leadership and, for that matter, McGregor's Theory Y.

### Herzberg

Herzberg is best known for his 'Two Factors' Theory of Motivation, where one set of factors (Dissatisfaction or Hygiene Factors) were consistently linked negatively with job satisfaction, while the other set of factors (Satisfiers) were linked positively with job satisfaction. Important in this was that high ratings for the hygiene factors did not lead to high job satisfaction, but merely to the absence of dissatisfaction – ie in themselves hygiene factors did not lead to motivation. Equally importantly, hygiene factors had to be sufficient before the motivators causing satisfaction had effect.

Hygiene factors (dissatisfiers) included such things as salary, working conditions, company policy, relationship with supervisor, while satisfiers involved such things as achievement, recognition, work itself, responsibility, advancement, growth, etc. It will be noticed that hygiene factors are to do with the context of the job and satisfiers with the content.

Herzberg's work has been criticised for three reasons:

1. The research method - because people tend to credit themselves with their successes and blame outside factors, eg company policy, for their failures.
2. He examined only satisfaction and not productivity and its link to satisfaction.
3. Again individual differences and needs were not taken into account.

Nevertheless, Herzberg's theory is regarded as an important contribution to understanding motivation. 'Jumping for the Jelly Beans' is a somewhat scornful description used to describe the way some managers thought extra effort could be induced by hygiene factors.

The importance of Herzberg is that, generally speaking, basic conditions (hygiene) have to be right as the starting point for motivation; they don't of themselves cause it. This fits with everyday experience where we know that such things are seen to be our 'due'. However, Alderfer has pointed out, at times of 'threat' we can alter our perspective so that security, for example, is given renewed importance. Generally though motivation comes from 'higher order' intrinsic sources, amongst which achievement and recognition are particularly important.

### Equity Theory

Equity here is to do with the ratio between an individual's job inputs and job rewards compared with the rewards others are receiving for similar job inputs. If these are not seen as fair then an individual is likely to feel aggrieved rather than motivated. The implication of this is that while allowing for individual differences (ie one person may enjoy being publicly recognised, another not), there needs to be a situational consistency about how people are treated.

### Reinforcement Theory

This is associated with Skinner and others, who were more concerned with the **law of effect** instead of studying inner motivation. The law of effect is the idea that behaviour with positive consequences (or good outcomes for the individual) tends to be repeated, while behaviour resulting in negative outcomes for the individual tends not be.

**Stimulus**
↓
**Response**
↓
**Consequences**
↓
**Future Response**



This led to an approach based on Behaviour Modification, which uses reinforcement theory to change human behaviour, involving the use of **consequences** to modify a particular behaviour. There are four types:

- ***Positive Reinforcement*** *– to encourage desirable behaviour*
- ***Avoidance Learning*** *– when individuals change behaviour to avoid unpleasant consequences*
- ***Extinction*** *– the absence of reinforcement for undesirable behaviour so that the behaviour eventually stops*
- ***Punishment*** *– the application of negative consequences to stop or correct inappropriate behaviour*

(Note – all of this focuses on **behaviour** not **personality** and **values**, as per the Onion Model)

Hammer developed this into some Rules for Using Behaviour Modification Techniques:

1. Don't reward all individuals equally – base them on individual performance, otherwise it debases the currency and offends the Equity Principle
2. Be aware that failure to respond can also modify behaviour – eg allowing poor performance, or not noticing good
3. Be sure to tell individuals what they can do to get reinforcement – in other words be clear about performance standards, what is acceptable and what is not
4. Be sure to tell individuals what they are doing wrong – don't avoid and don't confuse people
5. Don't 'punish' in front of others – for obvious reasons
6. Be fair – back to Equity Theory and Situational Consistency

It will be seen that there are many connections here with what we are suggesting in what is, hopefully, a more complete approach. An illustration of this is in Chapter 5 on Diagnosing Performance Issues where it becomes clearer that it is easy to inadvertently reward the wrong thing.

Critics of reinforcement theory suggest that it is too simple, and for some people the idea of 'behaviour modification' is unpalatable, partly because of the view it holds of people and partly because they fear the approach can be abused. This latter is of course true, which is why it needs to be applied under a firm set of beliefs and values, such as described with the High Challenge High Support approach (compared with, for example High Challenge Low Support), and as a step towards the meta vision of seeing someone becoming the 'best they can be' in a context of having Positive Regard for them.

In day to day terms there is little doubt that

reinforcement based approaches largely work (they are used much for training). Moreover in the early stages of the process, and perhaps where the Leader Developer is not yet in tune with individual needs, clear guidelines for what is acceptable and not, arguably helps people guide their own behaviour. It is more associated with the push style involved in Mobilising, and its legitimacy is in positioning the situation for Level II Learning and the 'pull' styles of Developing and Enabling. Here the issue is one of moving from getting someone to do something because you want them to do it, towards people doing something because they want to do it.

### Expectancy Approach

This approach says that the effort to achieve high performance is a function of the perceived likelihood that high performance can be achieved, and will be rewarded if **achieved**, and that the **reward** will be worth the effort expended, or in other words:

- If I do this what will be the outcome?
- Is it worth the effort?
- What are my chances of achieving an outcome which is worthwhile to me?

In all this individual differences and needs matter greatly.

There are clear implications here for Leader Developers, as outlined by Nadler and Lowder, which includes:

1. Determine the rewards valued by each individual – which means knowing individual needs
2. Determine the performance you desire – and being explicit about it
3. Make the performance level attainable – small achievable steps
4. Link rewards to performance – associate rewards directly to the achievement, ie catch people doing something right
5. Analyse what factors might counteract the effectiveness of the reward – clear rewards with no hidden penalties
6. Make sure the reward is adequate – if praise is the reward, give it wholeheartedly



Expectancy theory overcomes to large measure the criticisms of other theories, that is that all individuals and situations are alike and that there is one best way to motivate people. Instead it takes into account differences between individuals and situations. Its effectiveness is well supported by research and general experience, and it has wide application. It does however require managers to understand individual differences and have the perception and skill to apply it well.

There are clear links between expectancy theory and the process set out in Mastering Performance Excellence, particularly with the Level II or Developing/Enabling part of this process.

### Bass's Theory of Transformational Leadership

It was Bernard Bass who first contrasted two types of leadership; transactional and transformational. As has been said, transactional is concerned with determining what needs to be done to achieve goals, classify the requirements and get people to expend the necessary effort. Transformational leadership on the other hand, 'motivates us to achieve more than we originally expected we could', through their personal vision and energy and by connecting with our higher order needs (Maslow et al).

Bass argues that transactional leadership is helpful and useful, but up to a point. However, to be fully effective, particularly in today's organisational world, more is needed and that is where transformational leadership is required. In our language it is the difference between push and pull, between mobilising and enabling.

Boyd refined Bass's transformational leadership theory in terms of 'new' leadership skills required. According to Boyd these are:

- *Anticipating skills – in a constantly changing situation*
- *Visioning – including the use of persuasion and example*
- *Relating – being in touch with individuals' needs and motivations*
- *Empowerment skills – involving the willingness to share power and to do so effectively*
- *Self understanding skills and frameworks – within which leaders understand both their own needs and goals and those of other people*

It will be noticed that there is much linkage here between the competencies we have described in the transformational phase of Leading and Developing High Performance. Further Boyd argues strongly that leaders are 'made', through training – ie the skills needed are identifiable although complex, and amenable to training, and it is not just a case of being 'born' with them.

House makes much the same point as Bass and Boyd, but talks of Charismatic Leadership. He describes it as 'communicating a vision or higher level ("transcendent") goal which captures the commitment and energy of people'. Such leaders centre an 'image' of what is success and competence, and exemplify in their own behaviour the values that they espouse. They also communicate high expectations and confidence that people will perform up to those expectations.

It is perhaps a pity that this is labelled by House as charismatic leadership, with the grandiosity this implies and its distance from the way most managers would see themselves and their capabilities. It is basically the transformational stage of Mastering High Performance, and again performance can be enhanced through training and understanding, but it neglects the mobilising or transactional stage, and on that basis alone it cannot be said to be complete.

There is also, in all this, one other crucial point. This is to do with the type of vision leaders aspire to, whether they are called transformational, charismatic or whatever. Some such leaders have achieved much good, others much tragedy; having and bringing about a vision does not of itself guarantee that the vision is a legitimate one. This is why, as well as the practical reasons which give it effect, Leading and Developing High Performance is firmly anchored in a value set which emphasises Challenge and Support, Positive Regard and

Genuineness, and with a meta vision of helping people to become the best they can be in terms of their capability.

### Hersey and Blanchard's Situational Leadership Theory

This is one of the best known of the 'contingency' models of leadership. The term contingency describes the view that the approach that will best contribute to the achievement of goals might vary in different types of situations or circumstances – in other words 'horses for courses'.

In essence the argument is that leaders should adjust their leadership style to meet a team member's evolving desire for achievement, ability and willingness to accept responsibility – the Can Do and Will Do factors we have described. The Hersey & Blanchard model is a four stage one, as follows, and it will be noticed that the two axis of the model are Task Behaviour (Providing Guidance) and Relationship Behaviour (Providing Supportive Behaviour):

High

**Relationship Behaviour** (Providing Supportive Behaviour)

| | |
|---|---|
| High Relationship & Low Task 3 | High Task & High Relationship 2 |
| 4 Low Relationship & Low Task | 1 High Task & Low Relationship |

Low ← **Task Behaviour** (Providing Guidance) → High

The situational leadership theory has received much interest because it describes a leadership approach which is dynamic and flexible rather than static. The motivation, experience and ability of team members must be constantly assessed to see what style is appropriate under changing circumstances. If the style is appropriate then, according to Hersey & Blanchard, it will not only motivate employees but help move them towards the next stage of development. **Thus the manager who wants to develop people, increase their confidence and help them learn will have to shift style constantly.**

The main differences between the Hersey & Blanchard model and the way we have chosen to develop it concerns the underlying value set of High Challenge-High Support, with its attendant behaviours of Positive Regard, Genuineness, etc. It is firstly one of intensity of commitment for Leading and Developing High Performance, secondly, and importantly, Support is there throughout, it is expressed in different ways according to the stage of development of the individual. At its extreme level of **1** of Hersey & Blanchard it could be seen as High Challenge-Low Support (ie Low Relationship) and level **4** as the same. In level **4** they are not 'on their own' even if a task is fully delegated to them, and the amount of support and encouragement is still present though different in kind.

There are too some practical issues about situational leadership, largely concerned with whether managers can flex their style to deal with differing situations, or whether it is better, for example as argued by Fiedler, to recognise that this is difficult to do and to appoint managers to fit particular situations. Experience in the UK suggests that preferred styles are **2** and **3**, but equally the experience is that most managers are capable, through training, to increase their style flexibility.

**Organisational Culture**

Organisational Culture is a very strong force, perhaps often the most important one, in shaping how an organisation actually works, performs and behaves. What it is is a set of important understandings members share, such as norms, attitudes, values and beliefs. Schein defines it as 'The way things are done around here'.

In many ways culture can be compared with an iceberg in that while certain aspects of the organisation – eg its structure, policies and procedures are readily visible, what is less visible, and perhaps of greater mass, is the way things are really done around here. Clearly Strategy and Culture need to be aligned for full organisational effectiveness, which is why in recent years, when market conditions have required a change in strategy – eg customer responsiveness - organisations have paid attention to modifying their culture to support the strategy.

Part of this has been the realisation that in a fast moving world, organisations cannot legislate and prescribe everything their employees should do to cope with new circumstances. This is why there is an increasing emphasis on values as the guiding principles on which to act. The direction of cultural change in many organisations has been towards encouraging interdependence rather than dependence, and 'empowerment' rather than prescriptive direction.

One body of work had a particular impact in focusing attention on the importance of culture as a determinant of organisational success. This was Peters and Waterman's 'In Search of Excellence'. The book described the key factor – culture - in explaining the success of some major organisations. Among the cultural factors listed were, a bias for action, being close to the customer, autonomy and entrepreneurship, productivity through people, hands on value driven, sticking to the knitting, simple form less staff, and being simultaneously both 'loose' and 'tight' in structuring things.

However, Peters and Waterman made the point that companies with strong cultures that are focused externally – that is centred on service to the customer – may in fact be more sensitive to environmental changes and better able to adapt quickly than companies without strong cultures. In the event, many of the companies studied encountered severe difficulties when the environment did change shortly after. This introduces two important points about culture, firstly that the cultural factors described by Peters and Waterman cannot be taken as the recipe for success for all companies at all times, but that the culture needs to fit the needs of a particular organisation. Secondly, 'strong' cultures, through a success factor at one stage can become a liability if conditions change, and the very strength of a culture can make it more difficult to change.

How does a High Challenge-High Support culture fit with this? Basically it is concerned with keeping people fit and capable of dealing with change, as is described in Chapter 10. The only constant is change.

**Our Development as People**

It is useful to look at the way people develop generally and also the reasons why there is sometimes a dissonance between the way people can behave inside work as opposed to in their own lives.

As a baby or Child we are, of course, entirely Dependent on others to feed, clothe and nurture us. Part of growing away from this state results in Teenage Rebellion where we test our own boundaries and discount what others have told us. This (with any luck!) is followed by Early Adulthood where we have evolved a sense of who we are and what matters to us. We also feel competent to deal with most of life and to function OK with it, although our main preoccupation is still ourselves. We see ourselves as Independent people, responsible to ourselves.

The next significant stage is into Maturity, where we are no longer just independent, making our own informed decisions and coping well, but where we have the capability to operate at another phase, co-operating well with other people from the security of our own platform of self worth, capable of taking their needs into account and proactively managing our own environment. This is Interdependency; we make choices rather than being driven by events or conditioning. This four stage process is often described thus:

| | |
|---|---|
| a. Dependency | Directed, nurtured and sustained by others |
| b. Counter-Dependency | Rebelliousness, taking irresponsible initiative, being preoccupied with self |
| c. Independency | Taking care of self, becoming inner-directed and self-reliant, thinking own thoughts, making own decisions |
| d. Interdependency | Being self-reliant, proactive and capable, but also being able to join with and share productively the resources of other people |

Not all people make this journey to its full extent, of course. Some get stuck permanently in Dependency, either by choice or as coping adaptation, some, few, are permanently rebelling, others are self-sufficient Independents who don't make the next step embracing the potential richness of others.

Often, as mentioned, there is a dissonance between behaviour inside work and that outside of it. Frequently, this is because of expectations, the expectation that one will be told exactly what to do and be directed, that the manager is there to take care of all needs, and anyway s/he is paid to do so – a view often reinforced by managers under the Command and Control system recently employed. So people get habituated to this – if that's what they want that's what they'll get – and 'jobs worth' enters the scene. Other people see themselves as pursuing meaningless, boring jobs and don't invest themselves psychologically in them. Others, by default and design, find their fulfilment outside work. What happens, too, frequently these days is that people are suddenly required to operate in an interdependent, empowered fashion overnight. This is scary and a not uncommon response is to stay with what is familiar, particularly if you are not sure the organisation really means what it says.

These are just some of the reasons which sometimes inhibit people from operating to their full abilities. They may or may not apply to you but, once the choices are made clear, most people elect to strive towards the way of life of Interdependence.